Awakening the Light

A Survivors to Thrivers Going-Forward Story

TAMBRY HARRIS

SPARK Publications
Charlotte, North Carolina

Awakening the Light: A Survivors to Thrivers Going-Forward Story
Tambry Harris

Designed, produced, and published by SPARK Publications
SPARKpublications.com
Charlotte, North Carolina

Softcover, October 2020, ISBN: 978-1-943070-94-7
E-book, October 2020, ISBN: 978-1-943070-95-4
Library of Congress Control Number: 2020915078

This book is dedicated to abuse survivors who feel "stuck" and want to overcome the limiting beliefs that keep them in unhealthy patterns; may they hear a message of hope and find a path to healing.

Reviews for *Awakening the Light*

"This tremendously healing book is something everyone can benefit from as they seek to identify their true selves. Section I describes the backdrop of the author's mental health through discovery to recovery. Section II walks the reader through tangible, character-oriented questions to help uncover and discover one's personal blockages, strengths, and pathway forward. It helps the reader capture experiences as he/she reads and, in so doing, facilitates real-time recognition of past wounds in need of healing. This enlightening book of hope and healing is a very helpful step in the discovery process leading to each of us claiming our stories, our lives, and ultimately, our happiness." – **Dr. C.A. Welsh**

"The move from darkness, shame, and silence to light, love, and freedom is possible when we have the courage to acknowledge and face the harm we've experienced. The author's stories and images of how God has been made known to her are compelling, and reflective practices offer real guidance in connecting to your sense of the Divine. Having spoken so honestly about the darkness, she makes it possible to believe in being surrounded by the light of healing love. This book is a true gift to anyone who has experienced abuse, anyone who loves a survivor, and to interfaith leaders who minister to them." – **LeDayne McLeese Polaski, M.Div., ED of Mecklenburg Metropolitan Interfaith Network**

"*Awakening the Light* is a beautiful expression of the author's heart and journey of healing. There is a helpful balance of vulnerability and openness with her experience, courage, and passion to help others through the fire and integrate mind, body and spiritual healing. I love how she weaves her theology throughout the chapters to further engage the reader. The use of intentional pauses to remind people to 'tap into the whole of you' is powerful as is the reminder to keep your candle burning to stay connected to the LIGHT! These 'mindful moments' teach people how to slow it down and observe their experience (mind, body, and spirit) without analyzing or judging." – **Leslie Kay Maitri Canniff, LCMHC, LCAS, C.H.T.**

"Holistic! As an internal medical primary care provider, one of my most repeated phrases was 'your head is connected to your body.' Psychological, emotional, and spiritual issues a patient was experiencing often complicated, exacerbated, or were the primary cause of their physical symptoms. *Awakening the Light* is a comprehensive, empathetic guide for all abuse survivors wanting to live a freer, thriving life. The author weaves her own story into research-based steps allowing one to bring light to ways their trauma continues to limit their life and ways to move beyond these limitations. She is adept in illustrating that one needs to pay attention to their physical feelings in addition to how they are affected from a psychological, emotional, and spiritual perspective. By bringing light and awareness to these bodily memories, their imprisoned significance can be released, allowing one to experience deeper joy and meaning in life." **– Debra L. Coles, MD**

"Bravo! This book effectively speaks to this invisible community who has experienced painful abuse and to a topic that is easier to look away from than to bring light into. As a therapist, I felt the flow of the author's understory blended well with her expressed desire to help people grow and heal. I loved the connections to other authors and thought contributors, which enhanced the points made in the text. I was personally stirred up by experiences shared and descriptions provided, which help people identify latent feelings and what lies behind them." **– Bentley Ball, MA Counseling Psychology**

"When she would ask me to pause before going deeper in exploration, I would think, 'This is where the truth begins.' She describes how she would grow strong when adversity pressed against her and she was figuring out how to survive. I realized that although I might feel at times I regress into my old ways, I am actually progressing because this is hard stuff and you won't break through it all the first time." **– Betsy, survivor**

"Child molestation, an old family secret, is no longer the victim's cross to bear. The author, Tambry, does an excellent job showing how her memories became blocked from this insidious act of violation. Unexpectedly, her symptoms, like any other victims of rape, would resurface involuntarily in nightmares, memories, and physical reactions, preventing experiences of joy and happiness to indulge in the most natural pleasures of life. Those of us who have lived in fear and shame for what someone else has done to us must speak out to prevent this corruptible violation going further unnoticed. I recommend this book to be used to further study how these violations against the human psyche have detrimentally affected individual lives, from children to adults." **– Rev. Gladys Runetta Lanier, Chaplain, (RET) US Army, BA, MDiv. DMIN.**

Acknowledgments

As you read through my story, you will see how sustained I have been with love and support. It is hard to express how much gratitude I have for each person who has been with me on this journey. I will try to make my best attempt here.

My family: I open by talking about how my story is interwoven with theirs. I have tried to protect privacy while honoring who they are and how pivotal they have been in my life. I will name my sweet husband, Randy, who not only supported the writing of this work of my heart but also thoughtfully helped me build it out to be more meaningful to readers. My daughter, Katie, has been a cheerleader for me since I started telling my story in public settings and has added thoughtful insights to make the book more digestible with her young adult view.

My Companions: to these loving women who opened my heart, nurtured my growth, and held me during the most difficult times, I am forever grateful. They entered my life almost twenty years ago and for the past two years have kept my efforts around Going Forward: Survivors to Thrivers in their prayers. They have encouraged me when I doubted myself, and they have given me tangible support while writing and editing this book.

My advisory team: these women came to know me in various ways and believed in my vision as I created Going Forward: Survivors to Thrivers. Each one saw how she could contribute in her unique way and has done so for the past two years. They helped me craft the outreach of the organization, built out our resources and efforts, and have been fundamental in writing this book.

My friends: these friendships span the years. It is beautiful to think that the men and women I mention in my childhood, college years, graduate program years, corporate years, and evolution years are still available and supporting me at this time. "This time" is one of no longer staying small and instead claiming my worthiness and voice.

My therapist: although our time together covered only eight years or so, her words to me and the work we did together still speak to me today. I am grateful to her for stepping me through the dark pieces of my past and telling me when it was time to "look into the light."

To each and every one of my supporters, you believed in me and saw the worth long before I ever did. I love you and am grateful beyond words.

Table of Contents

Introduction 1

Section I: My Story of Hope

Chapter 1: Framing 5
Chapter 2: Forming 11
Chapter 3: Launching 25
Chapter 4: Evolving 39
Chapter 5: Awakening 49
Chapter 6: Claiming 63
Chapter 7: Thriving 71
Chapter 8: Encouraging Thriving 83

Section II: Your Going-Forward Story

Chapter 9: Welcoming Change 95
Chapter 10: Honoring Your Whole Self 105
Chapter 11: Examining the Core of You 115
Chapter 12: Embracing Mindfulness. 143
Chapter 13: Describing Your Desired Self 151
Chapter 14: Claiming Your Going-Forward Story. 171
Chapter 15: Growing 179

What's Next? 187

References 189

About the Author 190

Introduction

A great author and thought leader named Henri Nouwen coined the idea of "the wounded healer." He believed that through our wounds and suffering, we can be of use to others and find the starting point for our callings. As we make our own wounds visible and available, they can be of service to the healing of others. In his book *The Wounded Healer: Ministry in Contemporary Society* (1972), Nouwen wrote, "And when we have finally found the anchor place for our lives, within our own center, we can be free to let others enter into the space created for them, and allow them to dance their own dance, sing their own song, and speak their own language without fear." That is why I wrote this book. I share my story, my wounding, my struggles, my healing, and my hope to step into my purpose. I intend to use all of me—my experiences, my background, the concepts I have learned over time, and my heart—to shine light into the darkness that surrounds sexual abuse.

I have always been an avid journaler because it helped me capture and process my thoughts and emotions. Despite this tendency to write, I never saw myself writing a book. When my heart was tugged to help shine the light into the darkness of sexual abuse and encourage healing, I found myself being asked to share my story in different venues. People could find themselves in my story and began to express their struggles and pain with me. They also asked, "When are you going to write your book?" I don't know if I would have had the courage to take this step if another author had not asked me to coauthor a book with him. In the end, it was determined best to have two separate books, given the power of each story. By separating our voices, I was able to give more focus to my passion, which is encouraging survivors of sexual abuse to come out of the shadows and join me in claiming their going-forward stories and thriving in life. I believe God gave me this coauthor and friend to guide me into sharing my story and voice more broadly than I could have ever imagined.

This book is written in two parts. Section I invites you to find yourself, or parts of yourself, in my story. I share the context in which I grew up and ask you, the reader, to reflect on your childhood along the way. We walk together through forming, launching, evolving, awakening, claiming, and thriving. I would encourage you to have a notebook or journal close by while reading this book to capture thoughts that are longer than the space given in the book. I would like you to have plenty of space to expand your reflections. Although my story highlights sexual abuse, many types of abuse exist. I encourage you to find healing around whatever form of woundedness you have experienced.

Section II focuses on exploring yourself even more. I take you through a process of looking at you, the main character of your story, and seeing yourself more objectively, maybe even more compassionately than you usually do. The second part also allows you to have dreams for your main character in this current chapter and in the future chapters of your life. I would encourage you to be as open as you can as you write this. It is purely for you. Later, I will ask you to identify your "supporters" and "resources" because I believe that is part of the success of true change. But that is on your time and when you are ready.

The last element woven into this book is the importance of mind, body, and spirit. If you are familiar with breathing and meditation practices, and if you are familiar with getting in touch with what is going on in your body, I encourage you to use all that you know and give your body and spirit plenty of space as we move through the thinking and reflecting exercises. If these concepts are new to you, don't worry; we will work on them together. I just ask you to open yourself to the possibilities of what this new dimension can add as you walk through the book and your life.

My final hope in writing this book is that it begins to create a community of people who are moving from surviving to thriving. We are all on this journey and at different points along the continuum. The website **survivorstothrivers.com** has resources and encouragement for you. As you work through this book, if you find that you need some clarity or encouragement, please reach out and contact us. We want to be a loving heart that supports you.

SECTION I

My Story of Hope

Welcome to my story of hope and healing. I have pieced this story together from memories, conversations with others, and my journal notes. I hope you will move through it slowly, allowing the experiences and reflections to serve as invitations to ponder your story.

I use many images, metaphors, and analogies to show how my subconscious mind often spoke to me and perhaps how yours speaks to you. Allow yourself the freedom of using images and metaphors to help you view the process of healing more subjectively. You are allowing your precious self to unfold and be understood. This can be especially important for those of us who see ourselves as unworthy or insignificant. The path to thriving is to generously give ourselves time to see the value and beauty that lies within.

"

With each raised
voice and each healed
heart, we begin to
change the culture
that silences the
innocent victims.
We stop the shame,
secrecy, and silence
and promote hope,
healing, and health.

"

CHAPTER 1
Framing

*My story is one of light, hope, and
healing, which is what I want for anyone
seeking to unearth their authentic selves
through reflection and vulnerability.*

~~~~~~~~~~~~~~~~

Why write down the intimate details of one's life and share them with strangers? Why risk that level of vulnerability? Why especially would someone like me—a perfectionist who habitually strives to stay small to avoid making waves—choose this path? I reflected on this as I wrote each paragraph of my story, simultaneously feeling the dread of exposure and the freedom of release.

Sometimes the motivation is to give comfort, encouragement, and hope to others who can see themselves in your story. Although each abuse story has its own details, the feelings of woundedness are universal. These feelings include confusion because the people who hurt us may have been close family members or friends, and it is hard to understand why a loved one would cause pain and suffering. **We each must be willing to do our healing work.** As I have moved into thriving, I have found that the next step of my healing work is to find my voice around my truth and be a light of hope to others. Are you ready to find your light, find your hope, and launch into that healing journey with me?

Another reason for sharing is because many people experience shame around their sexual abuse and think they could have avoided the abuse, or perhaps the abuser said shaming things to them to keep them silenced. **With each raised voice and each healed heart, we begin to change the culture that silences the innocent victims. We stop the shame, secrecy, and silence and promote hope, healing, and health.**

The physical, mental, and emotional pain from sexual abuse seeps deeply into the core of a person, leaving them wondering if there is a way out or beyond it. The complexity expands as our lives are intertwined with others who may not be comfortable with the reality. I asked myself, "How can I bring healing and wholeness if I stay in the dark and remain silent around the experience and the trauma?" I believe my story is one of light, hope, and healing, which is what I want for anyone seeking to unearth their authentic selves through reflection and vulnerability.

A potential difficulty is that as people share personal experiences, others may not understand the complicated effects of abuse and how repressed memories and feelings work. It is hard to comprehend something with which you have no experience. I write parts of my story's healing process to show how these latent feelings and memories can emerge unexpectedly. It is also to show how, if kept buried and in the dark, these feelings can cause a slow death, if not physically then emotionally. I always knew this intuitively, and it is being proven through science.

A study conducted by the Center for Disease Control and Prevention and Kaiser Permanente examined more than 50,000 patient questionnaires to define categories of "adverse childhood experiences" or ACEs (Felitti, et al., 1998). They asked 25,000 patients if they would provide information about their childhood events (Van der Kolk, 2014). Remarkably, 17,337 agreed (Centers for Disease Control and Prevention, 2020). This willingness to participate allowed the patient ACE responses to be compared to their medical records. Those with high ACE scores had links to depression, pain, alcohol and drug use, heart disease, and even cancer. The stress from traumatic life experiences takes a toll on your mind, body, and spirit. I hope that sharing my story will add life experience to what may seem like dry facts. I also hope it will help others who have experienced repressed memories, as well as emerging physical and emotional feelings, to not feel alone. Sadly, these experiences are normal and can come as your mind and body heal. My therapist once told me: "Your mind may forget, but your body always remembers."

 Pause and complete Exercise 1.

Helping everyone understand the dynamics that surround sexual abuse so they can be supportive to those around them is critical. Sadly, no one wants to remember trauma—not the individual and not society. Words often associated with trauma are ordeal, upheaval, agony, suffering, anguish, disturbance, torture, damage, confusion, and shock. We would rather pretend traumatic events didn't happen so that life can feel safe and predictable, even comfortable. But horrible things do happen more often than we would like to believe, and we must confront this reality. **Bringing light into the darkness that surrounds abuse is my motivation to share my story and my journey of surviving to thriving.**

I was aware of what this sharing could do to others and the impact it could have on them. My story is interwoven with the stories of my family. It can be hard to both honor your story and be sensitive to those around you. So many people express this dilemma to me. My heart wanted to be transparent to everyone as well as true to myself. That led me to having a conversation with those closest to me, letting them know about my efforts to share my journey of healing and hope. I am grateful to them for their love and understanding. As I have worked with many survivors, they have not received the same support. Many are not believed, even when the evidence is obvious. Others are told not to say anything because of a desire to protect the perpetrator's position in the family or the community. **I encourage every survivor to continue to**

Have you had bodily responses that surprised you?　　　　　**Exercise 1**

_____

_____

_____

_____

Are you curious about anything? Capture your thoughts here.

_____

_____

_____

_____

_____

do their healing work, own their truth, find supporters, and claim their "Going-Forward Story" of light and hope.

 Pause and complete Exercise 2.

What is your sense of the value of bringing light into the
darkness that surrounds the topic of abuse?

_____

_____

How does this speak to your heart and soul?

_____

_____

_____

Is there healing you know you need to do?

_____

_____

_____

_____

_____

What fears are getting in your way?

_____

_____

_____

_____

_____

_____

"

I am grateful that I
live in a time when
our society finally
understands that
moving on and
leaving the pain of
the past untouched
can cause continued
pain and issues.

"

CHAPTER 2
Forming

The childhood message I created
was, "Life is difficult, and you just have
to be strong and keep moving."

Collective family and life experiences define who we are and the messages we tell ourselves, either good or bad. Negative messages can become limiting beliefs that hold us back from the lives we want or from realizing our potential. One way I've learned to move past such a belief is to examine memories to find the root, where the belief began and where it was reinforced. These memories can be elusive, which I found to be true as I started writing my story. Fortunately, many family pictures captured the events, so I have some recollection of my childhood. It saddens me to know that only a few of the memories are my own. It saddens me even more to think about why that is. The fact is, I would not want to remember so much sadness.

I know some of the stories that were told to me. They create a framework for my understanding of my family and its history. One of the stories is that my paternal grandparents were killed by a drunk driver when they were on their way home from a navy commissary in 1965. My father was twenty-two years old, and his naval ship was in the Red Sea. My mother was twenty years old and attending the University of North Carolina's nursing program. After being notified by the Red Cross, it took my father days on various cargo planes to return to the States. His father had been killed on impact, but Dad hoped to get back in time to see his mother in intensive care. Not allowed to go into the ICU, my mother stayed in the waiting room for days. Fortunately, Dad did get back in time to say "goodbye" to his mom who could only move a toe in recognition of his presence.

My parents, who had been dating for three years, were married right after the funerals; thus, my mom could help my dad with all the legal duties while continuing her nursing classes as a junior. Dad had to return to his service duties, while Mom continued to take care of things. They had intended to marry but not under those circumstances.

Pause and breathe. Allow this to settle in. That is what I tell myself. It isn't just a passed-down story but lives taken, lives altered.

I have asked what happened to the driver who killed my grandparents. Nothing. It was a different time, and those things just happened. I have a huge heart for justice and fairness, and this story has always haunted me.

I feel a deep loss having never known my grandparents, and I have just a few items from them to represent the lives that they lived. These items allow me to imagine them in some way. I have fabric my grandmother wove on a loom for blankets, bedspreads, and draperies, as well as a few beautiful earrings she made from seashells and jewels. My grandfather was much older than her; he had spent years in the navy and married later in life. I've seen a few pictures of his time in the service as well as some of them as a young family. When I would complain about the temperature in my house growing up, I would be told of their small house with an attic room where my father and his brother slept, sweating during the summer and seeing their frozen breath in the winter. These are a few of the things I know about my grandparents and my father's childhood.

The fact that my father returned immediately to active duty and then later to the Vietnam War, unable to process his parents' death, unable to take the normal steps people take to recognize the end of a life, is unfathomable to me. As I write about my story, I have been encouraged to share my emotions, which is hard for me because, even before my birth, my family has a long history of doing what is necessary to move forward. **Life is difficult, and you just have to be strong and keep moving.**

This was never said to me outright, but I had that knowledge deep within me. Perhaps it is the Protestant work ethic, perhaps some of the Irish ancestry, or maybe it developed just out of necessity. **I am grateful that I live in a time when our society finally understands that moving on and leaving the pain of the past untouched can cause continued pain and issues.** I am grateful that what I intuitively know (that trauma affects our minds, bodies, and spirits) is being proven by science. It makes my reflection and my healing journey justified because, sadly, I do care what people think. I always have. This is part of the reason why I have suppressed thoughts and feelings for years. But I get ahead of myself.

 Pause and complete Exercise 3.

What stories define you?

_____

_____

_____

_____

_____

What have you always wondered about your family's history?

_____

_____

_____

_____

_____

What messages became ingrained in you, either explicitly or what your child-mind determined to be true?

_____

_____

_____

_____

_____

_____

Exercise 3

Things didn't get easier for my parents in the early years of their marriage. Mom made a life as a navy wife and a nurse wherever my dad was stationed, although he was gone on the ship most of the time. I was six months old before he was able to meet me. Again, it's hard to fathom what he missed out on—the birth of a daughter and all those early milestones. I know this is true for many military families and is among the sacrifices they make. My father doesn't talk much about his time in the navy. I think it is a time in his life he would rather forget.

I have a few memories of my own from my early childhood, especially sitting on the back screened porch with my father when I was around four years old, watching the rain fall. He would also take me outside to look up into the cloudless night sky and show me all the different stars and constellations. He had been the navigator for the ship, which made him the second in command. He could share that little bit of his military life with me. It was a special time of bonding for us. I treasure that memory of being outside, taught by my father, sharing something that he knew deeply and valued, something to help me feel connected to him.

I also remember various things my mother would make for me. I had fabric dolls with buttons to button, laces to tie, and zippers to zip so that my little fingers could learn. My mother, sister, and I also had special homemade dresses. You know the '70s pictures of moms and daughters dressed in matching plaid outfits. That was us. Mom continued this act of love later with her granddaughters, all adorable in their matching dresses.

As I have gotten older, I have tried to peel back some of the layers of my family's story to better understand the experiences, memories, and feelings. Each memory, picture, story, and feeling are a piece to the puzzle. My cousin gave me that analogy. He and I will share the bits and pieces that we remember while trying to grasp a semblance of the picture. He says he's still working on the "corner pieces." I love him for his willingness to explore with me. Being nine years older than me, he can tell me things of which I have no recollection—where I was, what happened, the back story behind the very high-level stories that were shared. This all helps things make sense. It gives a little framework to explain what I do remember.

 Pause and complete Exercise 4.

Unfortunately, many of these pieces are colored in pain and death. My mother had four siblings. All of them died of cancer. One brother died at age thirty-four after a fairly short battle with cancer when I was four years old. Another brother died at age thirty-five after a longer battle with cancer when I was nine. I know there was a great deal of pain surrounding all of that, yet I have few memories. I remember one uncle throwing me up in the air when I was little, and I liked him. He's the one who died when I was four. I remember the other uncle with the skin-graft scar on his arm that looked scary. I also knew my cousin struggled with his father's death and his mother's grief, but I didn't remember actually being there the day my uncle died. My cousin had to tell me that I was present when I asked him to help me fill in the puzzle pieces. I was with him in their home when my aunt came home distraught and terrified.

My cousin struggled with the loss of his father. At times, I feel very guilty that my sister and I were the only ones whose lives seemed untouched. Death was all around us, and yet it was one layer out. My mother was grieved deeply, but our immediate family was still intact.

The oldest brother died at age sixty-three—old for my family. My aunt battled cancer for over twenty years, finally losing the battle at age fifty-six. Another cousin had leukemia at age four and beat it only to be killed in a freak parking lot accident at age sixteen. Her sister died at age thirty-five after battling cancer for years.

Do any special "corner pieces" come up for you, memories or thoughts that you want to capture?

Exercise 4

_____

_____

_____

_____

_____

_____

_____

_____

_____

Another cousin and I would talk about not living past age thirty-five. Growing old just wasn't a familiar concept in our family, and yet now we sit at age fifty looking hopefully into the second half of our lives. Many people may not understand my survivor's guilt, the pain of my immediate family being the only ones untouched by death in this way. I am grateful both of my parents have lived into their mid-seventies, and we hope many more years for them. Yet being the "survivors" has a different level of impact as our core family came to hold the rest of the family together. We are grateful to be there, to provide space for others both physically and emotionally. **But when hardship happens to us, we don't know how to ask for support from our family.** We have to be strong and suppress our own needs. Was this also passed down to us?

 Pause and complete Exercise 5.

My maternal grandfather was the oldest of three children, raised by staunch Presbyterians and a father who was a principal at multiple schools. Their strict ways led him to run away for a time as a young man. The good news was that his strong belief in education encouraged him to go to college and get that foundation. He was an avid reader and lover of knowledge. This led him down several career paths, and as he would admit, he never launched into one for long or became particularly prosperous. Yet my grandparents made things work and were able to have a sizable piece of land and ultimately the ability to send two of their five children to college. My grandfather at times seemed larger than life. He was an elder in the church, was a certified Dale Carnegie instructor, and taught at some community colleges. He was gregarious and highly esteemed by people who knew him. He would talk of his relationship with Billy Graham and theological ideas shared. Interestingly, one cousin offered the perspective that my grandfather was the one often citing his accomplishments and relationships. I believe my grandfather was exaggerating to compensate for his feelings of inadequacy and even guilt.

My maternal grandmother was very ill the whole time I knew her. She had to have her spine fused around the time my mother was a teenager. Subsequently, she suffered from back issues and pain for the rest of her life. I know a little more about her. She had three siblings, and when her father died during her childhood, she and one of her brothers were sent to a Masonic orphanage. When I looked up information, she was at the orphanage during the most crowded time when so many lost their lives during World War I. Her mother did not visit her. I wonder what it was like, losing your father and then having your mother choose not to

How does your family deal with hardship?

_____

_____

_____

_____

_____

_____

_____

What have you noticed about the dynamics?

_____

_____

_____

_____

_____

_____

_____

_____

Are there ways you would want this to be different?

_____

_____

_____

_____

_____

_____

_____

_____

raise you, to be sent away to a place where life was very hard and love was scarce. She didn't go to college and instead went to work at a shoe factory and ultimately met my grandfather. I wonder how each of these things played into her depression in her later years. Her history of depression was something that I know little about, but it was talked about in conjunction with the pain. One cousin recalls a lot of worry around our grandmother's mental health and all the drugs she took. I suspect they were to ease both her physical and psychological pain.

Despite her health issues, my grandmother would gather people for meals. In her later years, other family members took over gatherings around the holidays and created special traditions. For Easter, we had an annual Easter egg hunt. First, the boys of all ages would hide the eggs, and the girls would hunt. Then the girls would hide the eggs, and the boys would hunt. Of course, the goal was to come out with the same number of eggs that were hidden from the beginning, but often the dog would find one days later. Every Thanksgiving we would come together, and in 1976, the family decided to resist the Black Friday shopping craze and instead make Christmas crafts. We lovingly called it "Christmas crap" because we would bring whatever we had and made decorations. To this day, I have boxes and boxes of treasured Christmas ornaments collected through the years. Recently, I did not put as many homemade ornaments on the tree as I normally would, and my daughter told me that it wasn't nearly tacky enough. I needed to go and put more of the family-crafted ornaments on the tree. These are the memories and traditions that continue to bind us and bring us together.

I try to focus on the positive memories, but in general, it felt like we barely got through one trauma before we were thrust into the next. There was no time to talk about it, or perhaps my family didn't know how to process pain or grief. I don't remember anyone sitting with me to talk about what was going on or how they felt about it. I think it was even harder as I didn't have another grandparent relationship or "side of the family" to compare.

Even though I didn't have anyone to help me process death, I remember Cindy, a cat-shaped pillow that my mom made for me. You could buy kits with the shape of the animal printed on fabric, cut it out, sew it together, and stuff it. I loved that cat pillow and was grateful when my mom could make me a new Cindy when holes were worn in her. It wasn't until recently that I realized why there was a need to replace Cindy. She would yellow and age because of the tears that I would cry into her. I don't remember crying the tears, but I do know that Cindy was my consolation and companion in my grief. I can imagine the secrets and sadness I would share with her.

I had a deep, tender heart; perhaps that is why I always felt for the underdog. I remember in first grade a child who wore a wig. I don't know why. I suppose it was because of cancer treatments. I remember being outside one day on the playground, and the other children began throwing his wig around the playground while the teachers did nothing. It broke my heart, but I didn't know what to do. I was afraid of becoming the target if I stood up for him too much. It didn't feel safe to be seen, so I shrank away.

That happened many times in school—situations where I was afraid to stand up for something that bothered me. In middle school, the gym teacher made us climb up to the very top of a ledge, probably four feet off the ground, and face the wall. As we stood there, trying not to fall backward, one of my classmates was trying to cling to the crevices of the wall. He was so scared and traumatized. He ended up dropping out of school because of a psychotic break. I felt so bad for him but didn't know what I could do. I felt this way through my school years—seeing cruelty that hurt my heart but not being able to stand up to the bullies, whether they were children or teachers.

 Pause and complete Exercise 6.

Did you notice things in school that you wish had been different? What do you remember? Exercise 6

_____

_____

_____

_____

Did any break your heart? What feelings can you capture?

_____

_____

_____

_____

I think about how loss in my family was shared with me; I was never helped to process it. At twelve years old, I found out my grandmother died when I arrived home to find the black car from the funeral home in the driveway. Another time, in my thirties, I found out my aunt was dead from a friend. I wondered, "Why was I not one of the first told? She and I were very close." My feelings and emotions were not first; I wonder if they had been considered. I found myself following the pattern of blending in and not making waves because it would not matter anyway. **My role was to help make things easier for the people around me who were in pain.** That was the pattern established back when I was four years old. I wonder, through the years, did I ever really allow myself to get angry? I did when I learned of my aunt's death. I yelled at Mom with anger for not telling me but then immediately felt guilty for adding to her pain.

I was told "you are too sensitive" by many people around me (that deep, tender heart I mentioned earlier). I learned being sensitive was a liability, so I tucked it away, along with the pain and loss I felt, and compartmentalized it to move into more acceptable ways of being. I saw my grades as both a survival tool and my way of proving myself. At the time, I didn't see it as a way to address the underlying sense of unworthiness I felt. All I knew was that I had to do my best and excel, which was tricky because of the voice inside me that said it wasn't safe to be seen. So as the big, glaring "100%" grade came back on the paper, I would quickly cover it up so as not to expose myself. **Striving and hiding at the same time—it was a difficult balance.**

I had a sense of being unworthy in my friendships as well. My best friend in middle school had an absolutely horrible thing happen to her, and I didn't know what to do, how to respond, or how to be a good friend. Her father was found dead, in her house, from a self-inflicted gunshot wound. No child should have to experience this, and no child should feel the burden of trying to console her adolescent friend. And yet I did. My heart broke. I felt helpless and useless. I imagine I went silent around her. I had no skills around processing, no understanding of how to be present for someone in their grief. Our friendship drifted apart. I felt unworthy. My next "best friend" lost her mother to cancer. Again, a loss for words, a loss to know how to help, I suspect a loss of emotion to show empathy. I actually did understand this loss a little more but went silent. I was unable to conjure the words or express the feelings. I felt only guilt for not knowing what to do. We drifted apart as well. For someone who was told that she was "too sensitive," I certainly didn't know how to bring it to bear when needed. I didn't know how to grieve when two high school friends were killed in a car accident. I didn't go to their funeral. I didn't know what to do. **Once again, I felt unworthy and stayed small. One more pain compartment built out.**

I was able to find some channels for my compassionate and service-oriented heart. Girl Scouts was a way for my mom and me to share time together as she was one of the leaders. Earning the badges helped my sense of accomplishment, but it was much more than that. It was being a part of a group with purpose and caring. As I became a teenager this transitioned to serving as a candy striper at a local hospital and an active member of my church youth group. My church youth group was where some of my closest friendships were formed, some spanning through to today. Then there were the youth mission trips. Being able to actively serve and make a difference in peoples' lives while bonding with your team was an incredible experience and one that I continued into my young adulthood as a volunteer leader. **Here I was able to help the underdog, the marginalized.** I would not have known the word "marginalized" back then. I would have said people who are on the outside, perhaps looked down upon because of their status in life. Society marginalizes so many people.

Despite all the sadness, I did have positive high school memories as well— beach trips, sleepovers, secret jokes, being on the dance team, attending games, going to proms, and developing some deep, life-long friendships. Windows of awareness grew, and I felt understood, loved, and valued. **Like a butterfly coming out of her cocoon, my wings were spreading and my beauty beginning to come forth.**

 Pause and complete Exercise 7.

What are some of your cherished childhood moments
or memories?

Could you see the potential that lay within you?

"

Like a butterfly
coming out of her
cocoon, my wings
were spreading and
my beauty beginning
to come forth.

"

"
I had come back
home at age
twenty-two broken
but not shattered;
I was ready for
the mending. I
was learning how
to ask for help.
"

CHAPTER 3
Launching

I believe many women have
had their lives altered by abuse.

~~~~~~~~~~~

Every person is a combination of their innate personality, the accumulation of their experiences, and the mindsets that have been developed from actions that have worked for them and not worked for them. **Our core and limiting beliefs play into our thinking and decisions even when we do not realize it. Being blind to these influences can affect our lives and the lives of others around us. Over time, as we see the interworking of our mindsets and our actions, we learn to claim our power and leave destructive situations.** Unfortunately, sometimes it takes years of learning the hard way before we can see this path. Well-worn patterns will exist until we can look at them objectively and question them.

My pattern of striving for great grades at a challenging high school paid off. Being at the top of my graduating class allowed me a great deal of choice in what college I would attend, and I chose Auburn. This was a large school with space for me to thrive. The girls on my dorm hall became fast friends as we explored together what it meant to be freshman. I found myself drawn to a particular sorority, which helped me get involved with all the school activities, have fun, and show leadership both in philanthropic efforts and as an officer.

At the same time, I followed the patterns of staying small and feeling unworthy. One example of my staying small was when my friend came from the back of the house at a Big Brother party to tell me that one of the Big Brothers had taken her to the back and raped her. Another Sister said he had done the same thing to her. I reflect back on our response with regret and pain. We did nothing. We didn't report him. We didn't even kick him out of the Big Brothers. He was an upper classman, and we were freshmen. Who would believe us? I also think I went to a place of denial. I chose to stay small and silent. And yet, how many other Sisters, how many other women did he hurt? **Our collective voices would have had power if we had chosen to be seen and heard.**

 Pause and complete Exercise 8.

While in college, I met someone who was very charismatic and seemed larger than life. He had been a college football player and had just gotten out of the marines' military police with muscles to spare. We were both attracted to each other, and I felt fortunate that he chose to date me. We dated a couple of years before getting engaged. At that time, I had some people ask me, "Are you sure you really want to marry him?" There were signs of a darker side to him, but I felt like things were already set in motion, so I needed to follow through on my commitment. Also, this charismatic guy had chosen me. Wasn't I the lucky one? My unworthiness belief filtered out the reality of his character and what a life with him would look like. We were married and moved to Houston, half a country away from family and friends. The abuse began on the honeymoon. As the gravity of my life decision became clear, I sat out on the deck of the beach house with my tears blending with the rain that fell around me.

We had moved to Houston for me to earn my doctoral degree and for him to finish his undergraduate work. The dynamics were such that I was earning the money through the graduate program and was part of an elite group of students who were considered almost peers with the professors. This did not bode well for my alpha male of a husband, and he had to put me in my place, mostly mentally and emotionally. As I made it through each day, each week, each month, **I would silently celebrate the milestones of surviving his abuse.** When he would yell, berate, and threaten me, I would sit clenching my fists, feeling my nails digging into my skin, seeking to transfer the pain that surged within me to the outside where I felt it physically.

The situation of being newly married in a doctoral program was complex. I was completely overwhelmed with both the volume of reading—if you stacked the books and the articles, it would have risen to two to three feet high—and the fact that everything we knew, or thought we knew, was challenged. I remember loving the theories of Abraham Maslow. They made sense to me, and I valued the insight. In the doctoral program, Maslow was challenged and torn apart.

What circumstances have you found yourself in where you wanted to take action but didn't out of fear?

_____

_____

_____

_____

_____

_____

Were there times when you were able to stand up?

_____

_____

_____

_____

_____

_____

What gave you the strength to do so?

_____

_____

_____

_____

_____

_____

I believe the professors were tearing down our mental constructs so that we would be the thought leaders and theory makers of the future. Similar to those early thought leaders who questioned whether the world was flat, we were to deconstruct current thinking and question what was true. Layered upon this struggle was a husband who also challenged, deconstructed, and tore apart my character and personality. These are the circumstances in which I found myself.

Nothing I could do was right, and being a perfectionist, I strived to do the right thing. I couldn't lay a bag down without it being in the wrong place. If we went to a gathering or party, when we arrived home, all my actions were evaluated and criticized: how much I smiled, what I said, whom I engaged with, how long I talked to a person. And that was the easy part. That was when there was no anger attached. With the anger came cussing, yelling, degrading comments, and even having things thrown at me. At times, I would think that if he would just hit me, then the damage could be visible. One time, we were in my small compact car, and he reached across as if to hit me and hit the window glass instead. I was so afraid it would shatter with the power behind his punch.

Even when I tried to bridge what seemed like a huge abyss, I would be punished. One night, I stayed up late waiting for him to come home from who knows where. I wanted to try to have intimacy, wanted to try to be a normal married couple. When he arrived home very drunk, the anger and the hateful words just spewed from his mouth. With each angry, hateful word, another stone was placed around my heart to try to protect it. With each stone placed, I became more numb, less me, more a shell of a person.

When you wall yourself off in this way to protect that precious part of you, you certainly don't want to be touched by the person whose attack led to the creation of that wall. How can you be intimate with someone who terrorizes you? Yet, he insisted that sex was my duty as his wife and would force himself on me. The good yet sad thing is that I knew how to "go away" in my head and leave my body. I learned that at an early age.

When he was done with the conquering, I would move to the farthest edge of the bed and cry. In some ways, I was making myself small again. I was taking up as little space as I could and at the same time wrapping myself up with whatever loving reserves I had within me. It was decades before I could name this experience for what it really was: rape. Although the tears that ran down my face should have told me this, it was hard to admit. This is not unique to me. Many women have been or are in relationships where the expectation of sex is placed on them, and they find themselves either giving in or being forced into it. This brings an unhealthy sense of helplessness into the relationship.

I have been asked my sense of where God was in both my childhood and this situation. My sense is that God was crying with me, hurting with me, struggling with me. Through all of this, I did not lose my connection with God. God was with me when I would sit holding myself together, wondering if I could make it through another day of this marriage. I would often drive across town to a friend's house to escape my husband's abuse. On the way, I would think, "If I just kept driving straight and hit that tree, it would all be over." In my desolation, I knew that having that friend to escape to was a gift and an oasis. Even in the times when I looked in the mirror barely recognizing myself for the swollen eyes and red, tear-stained face, I still saw light within me. I think that was God's light still shining even with the outer shell of me so worn and dimmed.

 Pause and complete Exercise 9.

After six months, I couldn't take it anymore. My body started shutting down, and I could no longer ignore the impact of an abusive marriage. I decided that God would rather have me divorced than deceased. I had not let my mother come visit me in Houston because I was afraid to let her see what had happened and how bad things were for me. Although I hid the reality in our telephone calls, I knew that in person, I would have no way to hide my pain. When she did come to visit, I knew what needed to happen—find a way to leave him and transition back home. **As the tears and truth flowed out, I knew she would help me reclaim my life.**

When I left him and Houston, I also changed the trajectory of my life. I was on track to graduate from the University of Houston with a doctorate in industrial/ organizational psychology, probably working for NASA or somewhere like that. Yet by escaping my abuser, I had to leave that course, that path I had set for myself. I'm not saying that the path I took was bad or even less desirable. I was able to get my master's degree in the same field of study, start with a great job at Duke Energy, become a business consultant for Arthur Andersen, and then work for First Union/Wachovia (the names before the Wells Fargo merger) with some great senior leaders helping them develop their organizations, their teams, and themselves. Each of these steps allowed me to reclaim myself and craft my career in ways that fed me. **But I think about how many women have had their lives altered by abuse.**

Have you found yourself in unhealthy relationships?
What kept you stuck?

Have you been able to look at those things that led to that situation?
What have you learned?

What "oasis" is available to you?

Again, I get ahead of myself; much happened in my twenties. Returning home to Charlotte allowed me to replant my feet, reestablish myself, and begin healing from the trauma I experienced in Houston. It was then that my father was able to show how much he loved me. In the past, he would let me know he was thinking about me by sending a note to me in college with some article I would be interested in and sign it "The Phantom." Now, his crushed daughter needed more than an article; she needed the force of a father's protective love. After I returned home, it was clear what had happened to me emotionally and physically. My soon-to-be ex-husband did not accept our separation and came caveman-like to the backdoor of my parents' house. I wrapped myself up in a ball on the couch, terrified of what was coming next. To see my 5'6" father blocking my 6'2" soon-to-be ex-husband at the door of the house with a clarity I had never seen was heartening. I felt my father's emotions and devotion to me—things he had not been able to show before. I think the whole experience melted him a little bit, and he knew how to be there for me in that way. **I had come back home at age twenty-two broken but not shattered; I was ready for the mending. I was learning how to ask for help.**

My parents and I sat around a restaurant table creating the separation plan—not just how to divide the few things that had been acquired in the short marriage, but also how to navigate the murky waters that lay ahead. We come together well in difficulty. I knew they had my back, and I found strength from this. Together, we persevered, and I was able to reconstruct my life.

 Pause and complete Exercise 10.

My personal drive served me well as I enrolled in the master's program at UNC Charlotte, established a paid internship at Duke Energy, and got back on my feet. In some ways, I was building back the protective shell so that I couldn't be hurt again. **By being busy, I didn't have time to think and could define myself in my credentials. I didn't realize how I was falling back into a familiar pattern.** I moved quickly into business consulting and, because of my unusual background, found constant work on many key projects for Fortune 100 companies. Again, I found admiration in all my *doing*. Who had time for *being*? And is that really safe anyway?

Sadly, pain and wounds raised their heads no matter how busy I was. Ever since my failed marriage, I felt destined for doubt and confusion with broken dreams that I was afraid to mend for fear of being shattered again, being victimized again. But was this really living, or was it just surviving? I knew I was just surviving. I wanted to live, but I didn't know how. I began to see the pain in a positive way because it was an awakening to my life of routine and busyness. I smile as I think that being "busy" is the foundation of work (business). **By staying busy I didn't have time to feel or care for other aspects of life. It served as a nice insulation technique. Yet I wanted to feel and care.**

As I began to feel and care, the dam broke, and tears flowed. I realized I had never allowed anyone to go out of their way for me and tried not to depend on anyone. The one man whom I had allowed to be that person for me completely attacked me. Why would I ever want someone in that role again—friend, family, or lover? I never wanted to be trouble to anyone. I didn't want to ask for anything. My mindset was that if they help me, they will wonder why they are doing it, because I am not worthy. My mental message was, "I am not worthy of being special or even considered." **I believed I was this ugly, unlovable person that others would see and persecute.** That was what my ex-husband had done to me. Everything was my fault. I was the source of every problem. Everything I did was wrong. Everything I was, was wrong. I

Who have been the supporters in your life?

Exercise 10

_____

_____

_____

_____

Do you need to identify some supporters for you now?
What would that support look like?

_____

_____

_____

_____

deeply believed his words were true, and if people looked closely enough, they would see it.

At first, I couldn't figure out why I still hated him, why he had control over me. Then I realized it was because he was still there, in my heart and soul, telling me I was unworthy and bad. My therapist told me it was like I was a prisoner of war who had been brainwashed. I think it is the perfect analogy because I absolutely still believed the things he said. I had escaped but still had the emotions and fear wedged deep inside and reacted like a victim.

What this looked like was constantly feeling stressed and discounting my feelings. When things finally began to make sense, emotions flowed, and I could start processing, but I was very scared. Scared of making decisions because of fear of failure, mistakes, and being wrong. I had already failed in my life and made a huge mistake. I could not let myself be wrong again. I lived in fear that I was not really inherently good. Even though at work I was doing something I loved and was excelling, I was afraid it would all fall apart. They would find me out.

Pause and complete Exercise 11.

Exercise 11

Have you ever experienced the feeling of being trapped with unhelpful thoughts and beliefs? What were they?

_____

_____

_____

_____

Were you able to overcome them? How?

_____

_____

_____

_____

_____

Slowly, I began to realize that I had excelled to show my worth, and yet my worth was inherently in me, in my heart and soul, and not in my actions and achievements. These deep things were within me and must be revealed. This awareness is one of the core reasons I was led to write my story. I believe many people struggle with this "unworthy" mindset and need to hear that there is beauty and wholeness within them.

I began to understand that rather than identifying the symptoms, I needed to drive to the root of the issue. What led to these unhealthy beliefs? My mom said there was a sore almost like a cancer inside of me, and if we could target it, remove it, then I could be free. I was ready and willing.

To do this meant to be open and vulnerable. An immediate challenge was my mindset that weakness was one of the worst attributes you can have. Others prey on the weak and naïve. I had let myself turn vulnerability into anger so that I wouldn't be seen as weak. "If you hurt me, I will steel myself against you. I will hold my heart tightly to protect myself from the next source of pain." Does this go back to that fact that our family never had time for healing before the next loss happened?

 Pause and complete Exercise 12.

Over time, I could see that the pain in my family made me question the whole "life" thing. Do we just endure life, or can we live happy and hopeful lives despite adversity? I began to open myself up to more positive thinking: What if my hard times could be used to benefit me? What if I stopped being scared and stopped expecting the worst so as not to be disappointed? I realized that if you let hurt from others fester in your heart, it will continue to victimize you. I also realized that if you live life avoiding risks, you will experience nothing, impact no one, and have little meaning in life. If you're open to risk with life and relationships, you will experience pain but also growth, joy, and fulfillment.

I began to recognize that my feeling of not being worthy kept me from so many things. It would drive me to task versus relationship all the time. If I give of myself to relationships and am criticized, it plays into the insecurities. If I focus on tasks and work and am criticized, it is not about me; it's just something for me to do better. I was hiding who I was in order to avoid criticism. I believed that I was flawed and would be found out. I would judge myself before others could. I didn't express having any needs because I didn't think I was allowed or worthy. I was not able to let go of my hatred for my ex-husband because he took advantage of my unworthy feelings and did what I feared the most. He confirmed and fed them. Plus, he physically treated me as if I meant nothing. In letting that go, I could see it wasn't true, and I could see him as the malicious person that he was.

Working through all of this allowed me to date again. I began to open myself up to relationships. There were many personalities: fun, serious, outdoorsy, corporate, kind, and edgy. **The sad news is that I still didn't pursue the kindest people.** Was it because it wasn't familiar? Too good to be true? Or was I not worthy of that type of relationship? I still hadn't figured that answer out. Perhaps all are part of the why.

One man in particular was smart, kind, generous, and treated me well. His eyes showed the path to his loving heart, and I could melt into his embrace. So what happened to that relationship when he offered so much? My answer for years was that we both were focused on our consulting careers, which had us traveling weekly, and our relationship just drifted apart. Deep down, I knew there was a much more honest answer.

How do you see vulnerability?

Exercise 12

Does my mindset resonate with you in any way?

I still had difficulty letting anyone get close. I knew I needed to be present and open with others to show that I cared. I wanted to avoid my unhealthy patterns. I wondered, "How do I, this sensible person, take these revelations and transform myself into the woman I want to be? How do I avoid waking up in the morning and returning to my routine?"

At times I felt destined for doubt, confusion, and broken dreams. But I also believed God wanted me to live a more authentic life, a confident life where I was not afraid of how my authentic self would be perceived. I sought to embrace the idea that God created me with all my wonderful attributes and downsides that made me human and that I could be loved completely for the whole of who I am.

Pause and complete Exercise 13.

What keeps you from living your authentic life?   Exercise 13

_____

_____

_____

_____

_____

What gets in the way of you embracing all of you?

_____

_____

_____

_____

_____

_____

_____

> "
> I also realized
> that if you live life
> avoiding risks, you
> will experience
> nothing, impact no
> one, and have little
> meaning in life.
> "

"

Our patterns can be
deeply ingrained,
like a stream winding
through the landscape
for years wearing a
ravine in the earth.

"

CHAPTER 4
Evolving

Here I was again, initially feeling lucky to have been "chosen" by this person, only to find myself being treated as less-than and trying to be perfect and above reproach.

Our patterns can be deeply ingrained, like a stream winding through the landscape for years wearing a ravine in the earth. The course of its path can be altered but only with intentional intervention. As humans, we unconsciously and deeply ingrain our patterns and can unknowingly be stuck in them. These patterns define us and affect those around us, perhaps passing them on to the next generation. A great deal of research has been done and numerous articles written about our neural pathways and the fact that we can rewire them to regulate our emotions and thoughts, which of course impacts our lives and decisions.

I was growing in understanding my stream's course and the valleys it created. I was a work in progress as I tried to understand my patterns and their implications. At age twenty-nine, I married someone who was at least better than my first husband. I was attracted to his confidence, his presence, and the fact that he and I seemed to be on similar successful paths. He understood and seemed to appreciate my intelligence. He had a rough childhood, but I could love him through that, right? I thought he was "the one" when he listened and cared about my concerns when I was deeply upset and troubled. I felt seen and heard, which was a big step for me. He seemed to be there for me in ways I had not experienced before. He wasn't as abusive as my first husband, yet he still wasn't always kind. He still didn't give me unconditional love and didn't see all the positive qualities I brought. He frequently criticized my behaviors, and things were most often my fault. I would walk on eggshells trying to be the best I could be, so I wouldn't be reprimanded. **Here I was again, initially feeling lucky to have been "chosen" by this person, only to find myself being treated as less-than and trying to be perfect and above reproach.** My sense of unworthiness was being reinforced; I wasn't worthy of unconditional love.

Looking back, it seems that I couldn't date guys who were too nice, like I couldn't trust it. So instead, I married people who had something I had to mitigate and manage. I could help them and be there for them. Partly I wanted to help fix them, not seeing how broken I was inside. If I had ended up with someone 100 percent good and whole, if that exists, then would I have looked inside myself earlier?

Seemingly, every day there was something for my husband to explode about—incidents I couldn't see coming, so I innocently set him off. I saw a roach on the floor and mentioned it because I thought he would want to know and take action. Instead he told me it was one more jab and that he was "f---ing tired of it." He said I was implying that we lived in a "f---ing roach-infested place" and that I was a "f---ing whiner" who had been complaining all day. I sat speechless thinking, "Where did that come from?" I felt flashbacks of experiencing unexplainable temper. It felt like dealing with Dr. Jekyll and Mr. Hyde, someone who could turn on a dime with his moods. I started feeling like my world was shattered again, and all the self-defeating feelings came back. I didn't deserve and will never get true happiness, I thought. I should not expect anything from anyone because I was not worth it.

We would have conversations about his temper, and he would say he recognized his fault and wanted to seek counseling to address the flare ups. I was so grateful to him for being willing to work on himself and on us. I loved him and couldn't imagine not being together. Many things about us were right and compatible. I held on to hope that with increased understanding and his willingness to take responsibility for his part, we would be OK.

He learned to recognize why he felt anger, when the anger was coming, and how to step back to defuse it. I learned when to talk about things and when were dangerous times. Even with this and my love for him, I wondered how his anger and the resulting inflicted pain could be healthy. I still found myself walking on eggshells and becoming a non-entity, afraid to do anything because of the anger I would experience.

An example was when he helped me vacuum and left a rug outside the guest bathroom. I figured I could help and put it back in place. He hadn't cleaned it yet though, so cat litter fell out. A tirade ensued: Why didn't I stay out of the way? I was "making more f---ing work" for him. I tried to explain, but he told me to keep my mouth shut. I realized that I could choose whether or not to care. I decided to distance myself when he was acting irrational; this would be a tool to use going forward.

Another time he scraped a wall with the car and blamed me because I should have been helping him more. He was "having to live with Helen Keller." His tone made the comments even worse. I was scared because he could turn so suddenly with no reason and make me the problem. My way of washing the car was wrong. I went out the wrong exit of the Target and then pulled the car too close to the bushes. Another day he lost his temper, threw my purse and briefcase, yelled at me about my mess, and went upstairs ordering me to stay downstairs.

When I would try to explain myself, he told me to keep my mouth shut, or he would shut me up. He would look at me with such anger and hatred. I would try to remember exactly what he and I said, to be clear on my facts because he would be belligerent and twist things. I found myself yelling to be heard and developed some very dysfunctional fighting habits. I would try to be busy and not feel or care, to be tough like I had been in the past. But then I would have trouble breathing and feel a sense of emptiness. **There is no healthy way to cut out your heart.**

The feeling was too familiar: trying to numb myself from someone playing with my head and saying I was the one with the problem. I have heard the term "gaslighting" used for these situations. Like with my first husband, I was experiencing the same unelicited abuse with name-calling, accusations, and threatening behaviors. What was different in this relationship was that he would apologize and recognize the bad behavior and even be embarrassed for treating me that way. Of course, it would happen again. I tried hard to ignore him and buffer myself from the painful words.

 Pause and complete Exercise 14.

I stopped trusting my instincts and was scared to commit to anything I liked for fear of criticism and being yelled at for being stupid. I was scared to plan to do anything with other people because he would turn on me that day and not want to go. I would make suggestions of fun things to do, but they were met with resistance. When we did go out, it would be used against me in some way.

Have you found yourself explaining away bad behavior or trying to make things OK when they weren't? What did that look like?

Exercise 14

_____

_____

_____

_____

Why did you stay in that relationship?

_____

_____

_____

_____

Even though my home life was fragile, I found stability and value consulting internally at the bank and was able to do meaningful work. I loved the opportunity to get more certifications and strive to be my best. I wanted to be able to know more, do more. **My work fed me and my need for significance.** Others interpreted it differently, and I would hear people say I was "the one to beat" because we were ranked against each other for recognition, awards, and bonuses. This hurt me because I wasn't trying to compete, **I was just trying to be at the top of my game and prove my worth.**

During that time I realized my brokenness caused me to put my guard up so that I wouldn't be hurt in every aspect of my life. At work, I tried to be polished, strong, and competent. The feedback coworkers gave me around my performance was "professional." That comment stuck with me. Who wants "professional" on their tombstone? I would want to hear things like "kind," "fun," and "insightful," but I got a very sterile description. This was the wall I put up to be safe and not criticized. **Sadly, when I was my genuine self, I felt naked, vulnerable, and at risk.**

 Pause and complete Exercise 15.

After two years of marriage, a beautiful baby girl came into our lives. That was both wonderful and difficult at the same time, because it's challenging raising a child when you have a critical partner with a short fuse. I tried to buffer her from the worst of his temper and thought I could bridge the gap.

I would tire of being told to shut up, being accused of false things, and not being allowed to state my perspective. I was tired of being threatened and being called names. I was tired of trying to calm him down and being attacked even more for it. I hardened myself to him and sought to rely on other people to reinforce me and not devalue me. I tried to model behavior I wanted my daughter to see. At times, I felt so good about us and felt we were getting on solid, happy ground. Then it would be unexpectedly destroyed once again.

I did my best as a working mom, striving for a schedule that would allow me to spend as much time as I could with my daughter. There were swim teams, soccer teams, church events, family events, play dates, school events, birthday parties, and trips to the beach, mountains and lake. From the outside, we probably looked like we had it all together. I wanted my daughter to have a happy childhood, and I was trying to be the perfect mom.

How would people describe you?

Exercise 15

_____

_____

_____

_____

What would you want them to say about or see in you?

_____

_____

_____

_____

_____

Pause and complete Exercise 16.

At work, I was given feedback that I had a difficult time being vulnerable and admitting my weaknesses. I did live in my head and had been successful doing that for years. Suddenly, I was being asked to develop my heart muscle to be more effective. I struggled with what that looked like, but I was willing to embark. I knew I jumped to task quickly to ease any awkwardness in a situation. I would ask others to share without giving of myself. I knew opening up would help me become real and authentic. I knew I needed to take risks and reach out. **I wanted to embrace this new direction and show more of me. Yet I felt deeply that being real and vulnerable was not safe.**

Insight around this challenge came when my family went to see *Man of La Mancha,* a play with a deeply disturbing rape scene. Even before the rape, four men were grabbing at her, hitting her, and I felt anger and disgust well up inside of me. I couldn't get past this reaction to appreciate the rest of the play, even though I understood the significance of that scene to the plot. I hated every man on that stage, and I would not be able to see them afterward in the lobby. It saddened me that this play had been around for so long with rape as such a central plot point. It highlighted the timelessness of this issue. I think it was the domination and the helplessness that got to me. I knew my first husband raped me. I knew he psychologically tortured me. I was sure I had repressed memories. This brutal aggression I just observed in the play struck me as more than what I experienced in Houston. I wondered, "Why does this resonate so much with me?" I almost felt it happened to me at some time. **There was an inner knowing, but no memories came.**

 Pause and complete Exercise 17.

I would reflect on how I didn't want to be touched playfully, because it made me feel cheap. I wondered where that came from. I didn't remember anything from childhood that would have led to this response. At the same time, I wondered if something had happened to me to make me dislike sex, being touched as if only an object, and being suspicious of men. There were even times I would get a sexual vibe from a man and immediately have my guard up, because I felt I needed to be on the defensive. Nothing was overtly said or done; it was just a weird vibe that triggered and stressed me.

Have you found yourself trying to create the best life for your family but knowing deeply that, at the very foundation, things are not right? What did that look like for you?

_____
_____
_____
_____
_____
_____
_____

What good things can you see?

_____
_____
_____
_____
_____

What do you wish were different?

_____
_____
_____
_____
_____
_____

Could this have something to do with the recurring dream I would have about running from the monster? The theme was always the same. He would chase me around the house, just one step behind, and the only place I was safe was the front porch. I had to get out of the house and into the light to be safe.

Exercise 17

Have you ever had something like this happen for you, when you saw or experienced something that touched a deep place within you, and you knew there was something important to know about why it impacted you the way it did? What was it?

_____

_____

_____

_____

_____

_____

_____

_____

How did you work through that feeling?

_____

_____

_____

_____

_____

_____

_____

_____

"

I wanted to embrace
this new direction
and show more
of me. Yet I felt
deeply that being
real and vulnerable
was not safe.

"

"

My inner knowing
told me I needed
to move through
many layers before
I could feel free.

"

CHAPTER 5

Awakening

How many others have been covered with
layers of pain, sorrow, disappointment,
and regret? How many others might wish to
find the seeds of their authentic selves?

People can be like fish in water, not realizing what surrounds us until it is taken away. We become very accustomed to whatever "water" is around us. We are used to operating in a fairly predictable world, feeling like we know the rules of the game and who the players are. The water may be murky, but it is familiar, and we have learned to adapt. We have found ways to make it work for us, or so we think.

One fateful day, I was in a workshop where the facilitators were talking about energy and the impact energy can have on people. They asked for a brave volunteer, and she came forward. They asked her to raise her arm out to her side, and she did. They pushed on it a little to show how it moved down with a little pressure. Next, they asked us to send her positive energy, and we did. Her arm stayed out even stronger when they pushed on it. They finally asked us to send her negative energy, which felt wrong to me, so I just sat there. When her arm abruptly fell to her side with her eyes aghast, I had a panic attack, the first one I had ever experienced. My chest was tight, I could barely breathe, and all I wanted to do was get out of the room. I looked around at all the faces in the room, seeing which one I thought was the safest. I chose that person and pulled her aside at the next break to talk. Fortunately, she listened and understood and encouraged me to see a counselor to explore what was underneath this reaction. She wanted me to look into the "water" in which I had been swimming.

When I sought a therapist, I knew I needed someone who would not just help me work through my thoughts but also understand the impact on my body. **I could tell that my body was going to be a pathway to my truth.** It was what spoke to me in Houston, and it was speaking loudly to me now. In Houston, the heaviness of anxiety and depression translated into joint, back, and stomach pain. My body knew that I needed to escape from my situation before it took away my ability to move. In the workshop, the anxiety showed up in my shortness of breath, tightness of chest, and a whole-body urge to run from the room. It wasn't until much later that I knew why seeing her arms tightly held to her side was such a trigger. My new life and awareness began to emerge as I delved deeply to heal and grow.

 Pause and complete Exercise 18.

Another apt metaphor is a deeply planted seed that began germinating, the seed of my authentic self and my internal knowing. Over the years, the seed had been covered by layer upon layer of heartache, like an active volcano regularly spewing rock and ash. **Each time the seed would sprout above the surface, a new eruption would bury it.**

Then the volcano stopped. I was given space and time to breathe and notice what was within. I could dig through the layers of dirt and grime to see what was covered and to let light in. The seed could be fed and grow. As I discovered the richness of what had lain dormant, I wondered how this germination could bring beauty to those around it and perhaps touch the souls of those who could appreciate it. **How many others have been covered over with layers of pain, sorrow, disappointment, and regret? How many others might wish to find the seeds of their authentic selves?**

Other metaphors came to mind around that time of my life. Scales were coming off my eyes. Like cataracts, they had developed gradually over the years, and I hadn't noticed how they obscured my vision. They altered my perspective of life and of the people around me. As they came off, I was finally seeing more things clearly. Shackles were coming off my heart as I opened up to others about my learnings with vulnerability. I had closed my heart so tightly, I couldn't be honest with my thoughts, emotions, or wonderings. Before, I didn't think it was safe to share, so I locked myself away. But as I risked and trusted others, I learned how much goodness was available to me.

 Pause and complete Exercise 19.

Have you had times when your body spoke to you? How?

What did you notice?

What did you "know"?

Of course, when you unlock some things, other things can be affected. My repressed anger and frustration rose to the surface, the unpleasant rumblings and realization that things were not OK. At times my body would convulse and legs kick as if I were fighting off someone or releasing pent up rage. Other times my head would swim with confusion having so many thoughts wanting to surface but also having the protective part of me push them back down. If I objectively stepped back and wondered the best way to respond, I might have realized those rumblings were telling me something. Once again, my body was offering guidance and insight. Instead, I just wanted those unpleasant feelings excavated and burned away. **My inner knowing told me I needed to move through many layers before I could feel free.** As I lay crying with my own thoughts, it dawned on me I was feeling shame, yet I hadn't done anything. I had always tried to be so good and dutiful. A deep sense told me that the actions of others made me feel that shame and sadness. A thought came to me: "That feels so much like what happens to victims of abuse, particularly sexual abuse. Is there something I am not letting myself know yet?"

Do any of these metaphors speak to you? How?

Exercise 19

_____

_____

_____

_____

Do you have another one that better describes your experience? Describe it.

_____

_____

_____

_____

_____

It took years to unearth what I suppressed for decades: I was a victim of childhood sexual abuse. The awareness started with dreams and then faint memories of places and feelings. I began to remember the stairway to the basement. I could see myself as a little girl sitting on a stool knowing she was not allowed to get down. My mind protected me from many details, but my body increasingly knew the truth. **As the awareness revealed itself, things began to make sense.** As a young child, maybe five years old, I couldn't comprehend the enormity of what happened, so I repressed it. I am sure messages were given to me that it was a secret. Often victims are told they brought on the sexual abuse or that they were complicit in some way. I know I still have an issue being told that I am "sinful" or have a "sinful" nature. Although it is a tenet of the Christian faith, I know how destructive those words feel to me. **I think that is why I have always tried to live above reproach.** I have always tried to do the right thing. This would draw criticism from cousins and classmates. I was caught between never being good enough and being too good.

I am sure I was also confused because no one around me seemed to notice or recognize the abuse that was happening. **I think that was the origin of my "not worthy" messaging. I believe it was my child-mind trying to make sense of what I was experiencing.** I wasn't worth noticing. I wasn't worth intervention. Yet given the trauma and pain that surrounded everyone during my childhood, I now give grace and understand.

Things began to make sense. Subtle connections helped me understand why I felt the way I did, why I had trouble trusting, and why I had felt so alone. I was always shy and slow with physical intimacy. I was scared to get involved with anyone at school for fear I would get hurt in some way. The few boyfriends I had slowly opened me up to relationships. When I became engaged as a senior in college, I was very naïve entering my marriage. When my first husband would force himself on me, I would just go away, so to speak, until he was done, which came easily for me. I felt powerless to do anything, just as I had when I was little and had no control over my abuser. But I didn't want to be touched in that way. I wanted tenderness and love without manipulation. **As I realized this, I felt the sad, disappointed hurt of the little girl within.**

 Pause and complete Exercise 20.

My daughter gave me a figurine many years ago of a mother embracing her young daughter. When I first received it, it represented what I wanted for my daughter. My hope was that she could feel embraced and loved even when she was striving to be so independent. As I look at it now, I can see myself as the little girl wanting the embrace. Could I also be angry for having been denied that—anger around how so much death and pain could happen to one family? So much loss, so little processing, so much repressing.

People often wonder why others are affected by things years after they happen. **The truth is that if you don't deal with traumatic events, they will fester.** A hard, protective shell develops, keeping light and air from getting in, giving the toxic secrets and pain space to grow. Allowing light and air to enter will nurture the healing.

I was ready for the light and the air. I was ready for the healing in my life. I invested myself in healing and surrounded myself with others who could be a part of it, which is so critical. You must have others around who are able to tell you how worthy you are even when you don't feel it in yourself. You need people

Can you connect any dots to explain how you have interacted in your relationships? What are they?

Exercise 20

to surround you and believe your story, especially when you can't comprehend it yourself.

I had been "in control" of my life, driving hard for many years, seeking to excel, trying to use my gifts to the best of my abilities, and striving to feel valued and important, even special. When I opened myself up to healing, I entered a world without the boundaries of constant demands and activities occupying my mind and time. When I slowed down to open myself up to what God wanted to tell me and wanted me to know, my body spoke to me once again. More dreams came and awareness began to emerge. My busyness had kept all of this "knowing" submerged and unseen. Unfortunately, like a deep ache, the truth kept eating away at me. **I realized the life I had lived of driving hard for external affirmation was based on temporal success, career moves, and consuming projects.** When all that quieted down, I became aware that so much of my authentic self was covered and unexplored.

Ideas I'd heard before started to resonate more, such as the concept that you can't release something you haven't owned. **At first, I wondered why anyone would want to delve into and understand the past. Why dig up old hurts? Why live through it again? I realized the past would stay with me and haunt me until I looked at it, sat face-to-face, and then released it. To claim, own, and release—this was the path I chose.** I was in the "claiming part" for a while because, at first, I sensed things versus knowing them. As facts and awareness came forward, things I had previously sensed could finally be explained. I gained awareness that my family's silence and brokenness that surrounded me as a child "wasn't about me." The way people acted around me was not due to a flaw in me as I had always feared and believed; rather, it was the situation and what was going on around me. I could heal when I saw things in that light. I could understand and begin to let the pain go.

 Pause and complete Exercise 21.

I recognized I needed to go through the pain to heal and move on. Not looking at the past or grieving what happened to me had kept me stuck for years. **I had to work through and let go of the anger which was difficult for me because holding onto the anger and disappointment somehow felt protective.** Perhaps if I held on, it could keep pain from happening again or at least the ache wouldn't hurt so bad. I knew I needed to be strong and step out of my pattern and risk taking this healing step.

What do you need to begin to claim?

Own?

Release?

It took *years* of processing. Memories from particular years in my life began to surface as my daughter reached the same age. **I believe that in wanting to be present and available for my daughter, I needed to be present to myself, to the little girl within me who was hurt so many years ago.** There was also a piece of knowing and claiming the truth, that my innocent internal little girl had been groomed by someone close to her, someone she trusted, someone she loved. The innocence that was taken was not just physical but also psychological and emotional. I had to overcome the fear of what would happen if I named the abuse. Who might be hurt if I named the abuse? Whom might it disappoint? I had spent a lifetime trying to do the right thing and the good thing. **But how can goodness exist with silencing the victims and protecting the perpetrators?**

It was very helpful for me to learn that it is normal not to remember details and to be left with residual feelings and physical "knowing," especially when things happen to you as a child. A book called *The Body Keeps the Score* by Bessel van der Kolk talks about the science behind this fact. For me, it is valuable to have proof and evidence behind what I was experiencing. Things would happen to me that gave me insight into my repressed memories. For example, when my husband would kiss my hand, it bothered me. It was so confusing, knowing he was trying to show affection yet I pushed him away because the stubble of his beard pressed on my skin and triggered me. I felt a need to get away. When my therapist asked me how it felt, I said that kind of kissing was "yucky." This was not a word I typically used; it is a "little girl" word. My therapist wondered if this was one way I had been groomed. I was familiar with the term—it's when a pedophile shows overt kindness to build trust with their victims. I'm afraid that was the case with me. I never wanted my husband to have facial hair or a beard when he kissed me because it hurt. My therapist reflected on the fact that children's skin is very sensitive. I believe I am sensitized because of what happened to me. My therapist and I also talked about my levels of betrayal—first, the sexual abuse and, second, the fact that no one helped me, saved me, stopped it, comforted me, listened, or noticed. The second might hurt the worst, even though I know so much pain and suffering was going on around me.

As I explored the abuse, I remembered turning my head to avoid looking my abuser in the face. I guess at a deep, primal level, I knew that the eyes are the window to the soul. If he couldn't have my eyes, then he couldn't have me. I would not let him have my soul. I did the same thing with my first husband when I would leave my body. I would brace myself, be strong, and not lash out. Fighting it would only draw additional pain.

To move from victim to survivor, I learned the importance of owning my power. I learned how to breathe freely versus hunkering down, to use my voice instead of remaining silent. There was power in being aware of the anger and sadness in my body and what it told me. I began to understand what it allowed me to know and was grateful.

People who haven't experienced anything like this have told me they want to understand. It is difficult to explain, and I still have a hard time getting my head around how the awareness emerges. Memories and body responses gave me glimmers of insight into what happened. For example, I would have the sense of my feet running in little short steps, the short steps of a child. My inner child wanted me to know what happened, that she had been trapped and wanted to run away. The pain I felt was more than the early deaths that traumatized my family. It was more than the trauma from an abusive ex-husband. It was the repressed pain of childhood sexual abuse, and knowing and owning this truth was important to my recovery.

I became aware that I, like so many others, had been silenced, kept from screaming and claiming my voice. I knew I needed to stand up for the little girl within me in a visible way, to be brave and strong. I thought about what standing up for her would look like. I decided that it meant I would have a confident voice, saying when I'm uncomfortable in a situation or when something is not working for me. It means not glazing over my feelings by saying everything is OK. Being true to her, her feelings and her needs, is how I began to stand up and find a voice.

I continued the excavation. How many more layers were there? How deep, dark, and sticky was the muck I was wading through? It seems I had also picked up rocks along the way: isolation, fear, uncertainty, and loneliness. I held on to them so long, I didn't even recognize their weight. Yet the heaviness kept me from having a light and joyful heart, and any additional weight would feel like an unbearable burden. I tried to lighten my load—looking at each piece, understanding its meaning to me and why I allowed it to travel so long with me, and finally letting it go in a way that I wouldn't be tempted to pick it back up. When I felt a hole or gap where that rock was, I tried to fill it with healing things like kindness, compassion, love, humor, understanding, honesty, connection, and peace. I prayed God would give me strength, wisdom, and resources to move through this letting go and refilling process.

 Pause and complete Exercise 22.

Having resources around you as you move through your excavation is so critical. Of course, that means letting people into the scary darkness with you. That means sharing those things you think are shameful and embarrassing, but being vulnerable with people who are safe is part of the healing work.

My women's group, called the Companions, became one of those safe places for me. This group formed around a particular study. I had always felt a desire to "go deeper" in my spirituality, but I didn't know what that looked like. I was hesitant to sign up for a twenty-eight-week small-group experience in spiritual formation because it seemed like a long commitment. I had no idea what I was in for! This group of women shared, wondered, and explored deeply. None of us had "the answers," but together we came to an understanding of how God was working in our lives. What I grew to love about these women and the group was that we were so well rounded. We were introverts and extraverts who spanned decades, came from varying backgrounds, were single and married, parents and childless, and had many different life experiences. We honored the special

What rocks have you been carrying with you?   Exercise 22

_____

_____

_____

_____

Once you release those burdens, with what do you wish to fill in the holes left behind?

_____

_____

_____

_____

_____

attributes we saw in one another. We also shared in life together. Going away for retreats was special because it allowed us to be even more ourselves and laugh out loud at our silliness. We also developed a level of trust that allowed us to openly share our tears and heartbreak. The twenty-eight-week study morphed into a years-long group that continues to grow our faith. We have seen one another through a husband's suicide, learning a stepfather was a pedophile, supporting a child's "coming out" as gay, undergoing personal investigation over claims of a corporate whistleblower, supporting a paraplegic husband, year-long unemployment, career transitions, championing the mental and emotional health of children, navigating the amputation of a husband's leg, and of course, my "awakening." Walking through these times together bound us with a love I hope everyone can experience.

As I worked through all my layers of awareness, these women helped me overcome many painful feelings and unpleasant memories. Over time, my heart and spirit grew to meet my mind so that I was more integrated. Through the Companions' affirmation and support, I learned to be more grounded, more forgiving and better able to see myself and situations with compassion. Then came a time when they needed to love me through a deeply seated belief of which I was unaware.

Our group has a saying we share around our circle each time we meet: I am a beloved child of God—like you. When I would say it to someone else, I would emphasize the last part and not own my belovedness. Two things were going on here. First, feelings of unworthiness prevented me from accepting that I could be a beloved child of God. I absolutely believed that my friends were beloved but could not accept that about myself. One dear friend wanted to repeat it to me until I believed it. Sadly, when that wall is built up, it takes a long while to come down. Second, I was focused on giving versus receiving. **I was so ingrained in the pattern of being there for others, I had difficulty asking for and receiving help or support.** I sought to be self-sufficient but ended up alone in my head with my mind monsters. I needed to open to new things and make time for individuals who loved me, so I could be filled up with that nurturing love and support we all desire. To see giving and receiving as a natural flow or even an unbroken circle that nurtures goodness in our lives is an important growth area for me.

To this day, these women encourage me when I doubt my mission and are my cheerleaders when I question my ability to fulfill it. They will remind me of the steps I have taken up until now and how all these steps have brought me to an amazing place. Some efforts seemingly "failed," but they remind me that those failures have been woven into my purpose. I have learned and grown from each one of them.

Pause and complete Exercise 23.

Exercise 23

Are you able to receive support from others? What does that look like?

_____

_____

_____

_____

_____

_____

_____

Can you do more of that? What would it look like?

_____

_____

_____

_____

_____

_____

_____

_____

_____

"
I was feeling clearer
and more at peace,
as if talking about
what happened took
away its power.
"

CHAPTER 6
Claiming

My inner child was not only
wounded but also angry, pissed off, and
wanting to shout, "What the hell is going on?"

When we feel unworthy, we can't take in the good things said to us; we only let in the things that support the negative mindset we have created. Remember those neural pathways I mentioned before? Those well-worn ways of thinking may have worked for us at one point, but they can begin to hinder us from growth and becoming who we were truly meant to be. We must intentionally acknowledge and then challenge those mindsets to fully heal and grow. Otherwise, we will go around and around in the same frustrating patterns. Does this sound familiar?

At work my boss asked me, "Do you hear the good things that are said about you? Do you take them in?" The answer was no or minimally. It was a profound moment—her seeing my mental block and naming it. As we worked side by side, the eyes of her soul saw all the good stuff within me, and she created an opening where I could begin to own my worthiness. She also said she believed the company had done me a disservice several times over the years, and her goal was to build trust with me, so I knew she had my back and was supporting me. She knew who she was and could use her strength to nurture me. **Her words and her actions were light and love to the dormant seeds within me. She deeply touched my heart and penetrated stone to reach those seeds deep within me.** How much goodness and grace had showered me through the years while I sheltered my seeds from it? My feeling of unworthiness would not let in anything that did not affirm its limiting core belief.

I found myself needing to go back to the basics. A big step was seeking peace within myself and my situation. I needed to accept unconditional love and know I am beautiful, worthy, and beloved by many. When would I be able to take that in? When would I erase that deeply ingrained "unworthy" pathway?

Many people put written affirmations on their mirrors or other places to help them take in a new belief or way of being. For me, *when I was present and grounded*, I could objectively hear things that either contradicted or reinforced my limiting beliefs. **If a compliment or other affirmation came to me, I tried to slow down and take it in. It was important to be grateful for what was said and for the person who said it, instead of shrugging it off with a quick, insincere "thank you."** If a criticism or negative thought came from my mind or from others, I would also try to slow down to see it for what it was. Was it true? Was there something to learn from it? Or did I need to smile at it knowingly and give it no merit?

 Pause and complete Exercise 24.

I believed in a loving God who is present when you need support, comfort, and encouragement. That is something I have always relied upon. I can remember looking up at the stars as a little girl, seeing God in the heavens, present but distant. I certainly prayed a lot to him when I was in Houston, struggling with the commitment I made in my marriage and fighting to make it through another day. But all of this believing was more in my head and less in my heart. I saw God as distant, looking down from above, seeking to console me but not really with me. As my relationship with God deepened, the world opened up for me. **I began to learn how much bigger, deeper, wider I was when I expanded my spiritual life. I could feel God within me, moving through life as a guide and ever-present companion.**

I grew stronger in my sense of self. I grew stronger with my sense of voice. As my relationship with God deepened, I had a new sense of spirit. Those around me reflected back to me the growth that they saw. I was warmer, kinder, and more personable. People were getting to know all of me. This reminded me of the work exercise I mentioned in chapter 4, where we stated attributes of coworkers, and one of mine was "professional." Professionalism was a protective shield I created to protect that soft, hurt person inside. I was beginning to let the shield down. I was claiming a new identity and new words to describe me, such as authentic, passionate, caring, and approachable.

Do you have internal messages to which you are particularly susceptible? Is it something that plays in your mind, criticizing you around a particularly painful characteristic or trait? What is it?

Where did it come from?

How true is it? Can you see it for what it is?

Pause and complete Exercise 25.

I was feeling clearer and more at peace, as if talking about what happened took away its power. When I shared what I was going through with others, people supported and loved me, which dispelled the fear that I was inherently bad or would be rejected. I began writing my new path of confidence and love and sought to let go of the anger and disappointment.

As I continued to release the pain and hurt, I recognized my inner child was not only wounded but also angry, pissed off, and wanting to shout, "What the hell is going on? Somebody, explain things to me! Hear me! See me!" Giving voice to my emotions and recognizing that what happened wasn't about me or anything lacking in me was a big step. That left me a good, whole, valuable, beautiful person who could live authentically. I also recognized there are people all around me who have not been through this soul searching and who have not come out on the other side. I wanted to be present for them.

I began to create a new reality for myself. I recognized that my next step was to enter into more relationships where I was vulnerable and to share on deep

What words do you want to claim for yourself? Exercise 25

levels, unafraid of their judgments or condemnation. A sense of purpose had been developing that year. A feeling of increased understanding about myself, life, and my gifts emerged and felt like a crescendo where I was having more and more wonderful things and signs happening to me. The gift I received from all of this was a better sense of myself and the power of confidence to live my life, with God beside me, in me, being my authentic self. I no longer wanted to be afraid, or at least I wanted to walk through the fear with my head held high. I wanted to use all of me. I wanted to step out and expose and explore what I was feeling. The outpouring of support and love to me felt wonderful, and I felt that **I was reaping what I had sown over the years. I realized this confidence and positive sense of self had been incubating in me for years and was finally coming into full bloom.** I no longer wanted to live in the shadows. Instead, I was ready to use my creative and holistic-thinking nature to make a difference.

Fortunately, or unfortunately, when you slow down to be present, you become aware of so many things going on around you. As I learned of more sexual abuse in my family, I was a swirl of emotions, and I wanted to scream, "Enough! Enough crap! Enough of the struggle!" My tongue and throat wanted to yell out and not be silenced. At the same time, my ears and heart wanted to listen and provide that safe space where the pain could be spoken. Once again, I found myself in a place of trying to balance wanting to cry out for justice and being that grounded person who can be trusted with the truth.

 Pause and complete Exercise 26.

For one family member, the pain, loss, and subsequent addiction led to desperation and a suicide attempt. I often ask myself, "What is the loving and supportive thing to do?" After seventy-six hours of intense outreach and negotiation, we were able to find what seemed the best solution. We had literally talked my cousin out of jumping off a bridge in New York City, flown him back home, and with counseling support, gotten him to agree to being admitted to a treatment facility. I was exhausted—mind, body, and spirit—when I returned home at 10:00 pm. As I was getting into bed, my second husband turned to me and said, "I'm not happy." I was having shoulder surgery the next morning to address muscle tears and a bone spur and didn't have the energy to engage in that unbelievable conversation. The next day, as I was wheeled away to the operating room, he told me he would be there for me during the surgery. I thought, "Like I have been there for your three surgeries and so much more?" He didn't bring the topic up again for a week, which was good since I was coming out of anesthesia and on pain killers. When he returned to the topic, he admitted having an affair. We tried navigating the impact of this revelation, including going to counseling, but ultimately, he left the marriage. In the end, he wanted another life.

I found something interesting when I looked back at my journal entries from earlier that year. I had commented on the fact that we had just celebrated our fifteen-year anniversary and how grateful I was that I could share my spiritual growth with him. In the same entry, I wondered if he was just tolerating the interior work I was doing. Could this have been my subconscious seeing what my conscious self couldn't detect? My friends believe I had become too strong for him. I had begun to see my worthiness. I had begun to claim more of what I needed. Perhaps I had changed the balance of the marriage, and it no longer suited him.

The separation occurred as I was healing from my shoulder surgery. The irony is, that was the time I needed support most. The good news was that a solid foundation had been set. As my seeds flourished, so did my relationships with friends and family. A healthy network surrounded me, and I never questioned my worthiness. I was charting a new course with confidence in my abilities and my willingness to be vulnerable and let others help me. I was hooked up to an ice machine that pumped cool water to soothe my healing shoulder, and it needed refilling frequently. My mother and friends helped with

What in your family or life has made you want to scream out? What did you do or wish you could do? Exercise 26

that and with hourly shoulder-manipulation exercises that I couldn't manage on my own. This time, I couldn't be the strong one. I needed to lean on others for all my basic needs as well as those of my thirteen-year old daughter. But they were there for me. I was worthy of their love and attention. I grew to accept that truth.

My faith was deep, and I was able to be a grounded, loving mother, trying always to say and do what would be best for the situation and not what my anger might want me to do. The recovery took almost a year with complications that physical therapy alone couldn't address. In time, I was healed, but that was only the sprint portion of the race. The marathon portion was navigating the teen years with a very angry daughter who resented her father's actions.

My shoulder seemed like a metaphor for everything that was going on in my life, particularly in my marriage. Things weren't good, but I had learned to deal with the pain. At times, things would flare up and ultimately needed to be addressed. A very invasive procedure removed unhealthy aspects. Healing took a long time, way longer than I expected. I had supportive people helping me toward recovery, and I made it over the hump. I began to think about what my new and improved life might be like. I grew stronger despite the setbacks and knew I would be better than ever.

Pause and complete Exercise 27.

Does the shoulder metaphor apply to your life?

Exercise 27

_____

_____

_____

What times in your life have been painful but, in the end, for the best?

_____

_____

_____

_____

"

But for the walls to be dissipated by the light of God had so much more power for me. I was not left with rubble to deal with, only beauty and light.

"

CHAPTER 7

Thriving

I had lived in a dark and limiting box, but it was
familiar and therefore I had a sense of safety.
But this self-imposed box hindered my growth
in my experiences and exposure. I knew it was
time to leave the box and begin thriving.

As we create new pathways of thinking or expand our neural pathways, we develop new ways of being. At first this can feel uncomfortable because it is unfamiliar. It can also leave you feeling incompetent as you step into the unknown, but the more you try, the better and more competent you are. In time, you will realize how comfortable that way of being has become and how little effort is required. It is like the first time you tried to drive a car. I remember being anxious and uncomfortable. Now I barely think about all the steps I take to back out of the driveway. Over time, these new ways of being become a part of you.

In this healing and expanding time, I needed to trust God more and control less. Unfortunately, that was challenging because I was used to being good at what I did and didn't know what this "relying on God" looked like. I knew how to be an achiever in school and at work but had no clue how to engage with my teenage daughter and not try to overly control life. I knew how to be busy and get lost in the flurry. To be still, present, and release control to God was such a stretch for me.

As I felt so incompetent and lost, I reflected on what it would be like to look at myself with the eyes of compassion as I would with a friend. When I did this, I saw someone who had a large heart for family and friends, who had been through a lot. I saw someone who tried so hard to do what was right. I then felt God telling me, "Let me love you. There's no trying in that, only receiving."

Later, I heard a song that said, "Girl let me love you until you learn to love yourself." It is a secular song, but that night I heard God saying it to me: "Tambry, let me love you until you learn to love yourself." I still feel a tingling sensation all over my body thinking about it. What does it look like to let God love me? What if I let Him hold my well-being at great importance and take care of me with all of His heart? What if I let Him think about me all the time and know when I am hurting and in need? I also wondered, "What does it mean to love myself?"

 Pause and complete Exercise 28.

I reflected on all the healing I had done around the childhood pain and sexual abuse. It was a piece of the past that I no longer repressed with shame. It happened. I was damaged. I suffered. Relationships were stifled. But I had become strong. It no longer felt like a secret not to be shared; it was one facet of who I am. I am a survivor who is rising above it all and claiming life on my

---

What does it mean for you to love yourself?   Exercise 28

terms versus trying to exist in spite of myself. Before, I saw myself as less than and cowered, afraid that I would be found out. Now, I see and embrace who I am and allow others to embrace this multifaceted person coming into who God created her to be.

My dreams reflected my internal growth. In one dream, I went for a walk with God along a sunny, rolling path. God stopped in front of a heavy door to his right. Inside were the dark walls of a dungeon or basement. I cried out loud at the fearful thought of going in, but we went in together. It was cold, damp, and foreboding. He encouraged us to stay for a while, and I needed to sit down. God stood to my left with his arm around my shoulders. He gave comfort but didn't obscure my view around me. This was important because I was afraid someone would come up behind me. I noticed light beginning to come into the room. The room still had stone blocks, but it was not as ominous. Light permeated the stones, and then suddenly the walls began to dissipate. I was then sitting beside the path, outdoors. The room had ceased to exist. All I saw around me was nature, rolling hills, and a bright sun. I somehow had expected the walls of the dungeon to tumble down or be broken apart. **But for them to be dissipated by the light of God had so much more power for me. I was not left with rubble to deal with, only beauty and light.**

In another dream, I saw myself adeptly navigating white-water rapids in my kayak, years of experience making it easy and fun for me. I have approached life from a fearful place: What is going to be thrown at me? What will I need to deal with? To think of my life as a fun adventure was a wonderful thought and tremendous growth. I realized that nothing had been thrown at me that I couldn't handle. I have scars and have been worn down in places due to hardships, but it's like the patina on furniture that makes it interesting. I can have this patina and still be what I was meant to be.

 Pause and complete Exercise 29.

Like all healing, there were ups and downs, and at times, I was lonely. You can have friends and family be available to you, but that is not the same as having a life partner. One day I realized how much I missed my teenage daughter when she was away with friends, missed her even when she was home but locked away in her room. Loneliness and sadness tugged at my heart. Then an image came to me of pieces of colored glass. They could be put together into a beautiful mosaic but were scattered randomly and diminished. I looked at each piece and could see the beauty I would miss if I didn't slow down. It reminded me not to rush through this piece or this time too fast because I would miss the beauty of the moment. This was the hard work of transition and loss.

Other images came to me, for example, seeing the door of my heart. I could see beyond the door to the beauty waiting for me outside. The door opened outward so that I was in control and could go out versus letting things come in and overwhelm me. And I could go through the door whenever I was ready. When I ventured out, the sun was bright and warm. The flowers were colorful, cheerful, and brilliant. I knew a new season of beauty was awaiting me. As I walked into it, I knew this was a space God created for me. It had been waiting for me, and it was safe. It was a place that I could feel love and "just be." It was leaving the box I had contained myself in and growing into a new space. **The box was dark and limiting but familiar; therefore, I had a sense of safety. Yet it hindered my ability to grow through experiences and exposure.**

I shared with a group of friends that I felt a sense of purpose as I worked through my past hoping to be an instrument of God. What I didn't know was, should I volunteer somewhere, change my career direction, or start

What dreams have you had that might be insight into your growth or desired growth areas?

Exercise 29

up a ministry? I knew I didn't have the energy to do anything radical at that point. I was in a preparatory time of healing, building wisdom, and gaining understanding so that when the opportunity presented itself, I would be ready. My daily devotion said that by going through the daily routine, you are working your program, learning to love yourself, God, and those around you. This process helps you be fully alive, using all the faculties of your personality in every area of your life.

 Pause and complete Exercise 30.

Sharing with friends was a big step. By revealing what I had lived through, I had the opportunity to help others identify their experiences and dispel feelings of marginalization or isolation. Recovery and healing cannot occur in isolation.

Advisors encouraged me to just "be" and allow doors and opportunities to open. I also knew that I needed to find courage to continue healing. When I first considered this, I thought it was courage to talk fearlessly about situations with others to overcome what I considered to be judgment of the past. Instead, it was

What daily routines do you have that can allow for reflection into yourself?	Exercise 30

courage to examine and understand the judging voices within me. I wondered, "Is this awareness a gift I have to give others?" I could also sense a rising passion around stopping the silence that surrounds sexual abuse, the silence that traps us inside our protective shells and separates us from others. I read through past journal entries and saw where I had described stopping the silence and having people recognize the importance of owning their stories and sharing them to be able to heal. **I was amazed to realize the desire to launch my Going-Forward efforts was put on my heart almost ten years ago.**

I sensed my purpose was to use my experience to help others. I wanted to connect survivors to health and fulfillment, the whole of each person, mind, body, and spirit. I knew that God gave me the gifts of listening, providing insight, helping others to be still and settle into their bodies and spirit, creating a safe and nurturing environment, harnessing a passion that leads to vision, and making it happen with a loving and compassionate heart. A more practical gift was organization and the ability to get things done. I just needed to see what exactly I felt I was guided to do.

I tried to listen fully with my mind, body, and spirit. I also tried to trust timing. I had a sense that God had a better plan for me than I could have imagined. Maybe pieces were only becoming clear one at a time because it would be overwhelming if I saw things completely. I reflected that maybe I was in training, perhaps for the role of my lifetime.

 Pause and complete Exercise 31.

I found myself in the place of being able to dream and hope again. I wanted to think I could have a loving partner to share life. So what would that look like? In my mind, a partner would cherish me, gaze at me with loving eyes, and see the good in me. He would want to be on this adventure with me. He would want to know about my dreams, learnings, and experiences because that is who I am. He would want to know and love all of me.

Over time, I felt free to date again. I wanted my daughter to see what a kind and loving man looked like, one I could love with all my heart who would love all of me as well. It took a while to find him—or really, he found me. Remember the kind guy I dated in my twenties? We had worked at the bank at the same time and had connected professionally years ago. It seems that LinkedIn can be used for more than work-related connections because he asked if I would be open to meet him for lunch. Not knowing his motivation (how would he know I was divorced?),

I curiously said, "Sure." At lunch it was like sitting down in front of an old friend you haven't seen in years and picking up right where you left off. I quickly asked if this meeting was business or personal, and he responded, "I just thought it would be good to meet." (A response he admits was not the wittiest.) That open space allowed the conversation to go wherever felt natural. I found myself immediately comfortable, and we gravitated toward the more personal side of things. In that hour, we laughed, shared, and bridged those twenty-one years like no time had passed.

One thing that was shared in the "personal" side of the conversation was our reflection on our hope for future relationships and the importance to have all the "boxes" checked: physical, intellectual, emotional, and spiritual. In past relationships, I would check the physical and intellectual boxes with part of the emotional box checked and thought I was doing pretty good. To think about having the spiritual box checked really had never dawned on me. I have always been a deeply emotional person who knew she had a spiritual side wanting to be deepened. I never thought of a partner being able to be a part of that aspect. To

Have you had a sense of "knowing" you were meant to do something, but the specifics were unclear? What can you capture about it?

Exercise 31

Could you feel this in your mind, body, or spirit? How?

explore this with a man who also was seeking these things seemed too good to be true. Yet here he was.

As we began to date, I found someone who wanted to go out exploring new experiences with me. He wanted to go to interesting restaurants, listen to live music, and loved the outdoors. By our fourth or fifth date, we went to an intimate restaurant, held hands across the table, and began to speak our hearts to one another. We both had things we wanted to share that we felt were important to know so that our relationship would continue to grow in a transparent way. Neither of us held back. For me, I wanted him to know and understand what I had been through with the sexual abuse. Although it was something that happened years ago, the ramifications are still a part of my life. You see, he had a goatee. I have shared in my story how facial hair is a trigger for me. To name the trigger leads to explaining the "why" behind it. This is what survivors face, trying to balance their needs and the timing of bringing someone into the darkness of their past. The beautiful thing is that none of this bothered him; he held me and my story compassionately. Time passed until we were the last ones in the restaurant.

Then there was the "broccoli incident." We had been dating a couple of months and were going to cook dinner at his house. He wanted to make a broccoli dish, and I told him the ingredients from a recipe I had. I also took a picture of the recipe and texted it to him. As I was driving over to his house, a text came through from him. It seems that I had told him to buy one bunch of broccoli, while the recipe required two. My head started swirling, and fear welled up in me. I worried about what situation I was driving into. The words started swimming in my head. "I can't believe you are so stupid! Why can't you f---ing read a recipe?" As I pulled into the driveway, he came up to the car. I opened the door apologizing profusely for my error. He looked at me confused and said, "I just wanted to know if I need to go to the grocery store to get a second bunch of broccoli." It had never occurred to him to be upset about it, never even crossed his mind.

This may sound simple and silly. But any woman who has been emotionally and verbally abused by her partner knows what I'm talking about. She knows how you try to do everything so right, try to be so helpful, and yet something happens, you mess up, and you wait for the abuse to start. You hear the words in your head before they even come out of his mouth. That shield is up trying to protect you from what is going to be hitting you soon.

Here came a normal, healthy relationship, one that I didn't even know was possible, based on seeking to understand and support, where the best is assumed versus the worst. I was moving into a relationship unlike any I had ever known, where I could be vulnerable. When I messed up, like misreading ingredients, it was received with a helpful, "What can I do?" I learned that I could be all of me. The silly part of me who wants to sing out loud to ABBA and Journey songs, the deep part who wants to sit and journal when it is late at night and I can't sleep for the thoughts that are in my head, the fun part who wants to be inspired to dance at a concert even when no one else is, the intellectual part who wants to explore a concept I just learned, and the tender part who melts with a caress.

As we dated, all of the boxes were checked for me. He was just so darn cute with his bright smile and his eyes so beautiful and caring. When he hugged me, I could fold into his arms and want to be there for hours. I appreciated his intellect and his thinking deeply about life. His emotional depth matched mine, and he could broaden my perspective in a loving way. He shared his spiritual side, which had come alive after his divorce. There was a certainty that God was with him, operating in his life, and he knew that good would ultimately come after the heartbreak he had endured. Later, he would talk about how he knew God would bring the right person to him; his trust and faithfulness were remarkable.

This man showed me so much love and kindness. He continues to bless me every day, and I am so grateful that God brought him into my life. We are both amazed at the depth of connection and love we feel for one another. I am amazed by the way he looks at me, takes me in, and cherishes me. That is exactly what I prayed for; I didn't know how incredible it could feel to be loved in this way. After two years of dating, I married the love of my life. I finally got it right.

I smile thinking that God had tried to get us together all those years ago, and I was just too blind to see. **I really think I was too wounded to see. I needed to heal to be able to let someone so loving into my life.** You must love and honor yourself, value yourself, before you can join in a healthy relationship. The beautiful thing is that my daughter has embraced him wholeheartedly, and she is a tough critic!

The evolution in me continued given this new, incredible addition to my life. My husband's love and kindness helped nurture my evolving patience, openness, and vulnerability. He would often respond to me in an understanding way when I was surprised by or disappointed in my daughter's actions. I am sure being the daughter of a perfectionist, as well meaning as I was, could be hard. As I loosened the reigns and held a wider, loving container around my daughter, she slowly thrashed out less. As my ability increased to breathe and "be" in a moment versus react, she sparred less because I wasn't a willing participant. Her teenage self still wanted to keep me at arm's length, but an appreciative connection developed.

I believe she could feel my heart and my effort to shift my behavior to give her more space.

When she applied to colleges alone and limited the number of campus visits she wanted me to attend with her, I knew I had to let her control her own path. I had to trust her and God that it would be OK. I knew that the perfect mother might be sitting down with her once a week mapping activities and evaluating universities on a matrix. Or maybe for her, being the perfect mother meant allowing her to own these steps herself, in her way. Once again, I was a work in progress. In the end, to have her happy and thriving as she entered college was a dream come true.

Back in chapter 2, I compared life to a jigsaw puzzle. The trouble with that analogy, and with such puzzles, is that you may never find the missing pieces to complete the picture. **Perhaps instead we might view life as a mosaic where each piece has richness and texture on its own. When put together, they form a uniquely beautiful piece of art.** My husband and daughter are certainly beautiful pieces in my mosaic. It amazes me how many others have come in and added pieces or even reflective light to make it more beautiful.

Part of this beauty is having people surround you for years, witnessing your growth and reflecting what they see back to you. I told you about the women in my Companions group, which I have been a part of for almost twenty years, and how they have been an incredible gift to me. We not only encourage one another to grow and explore, but also revel in what emerges in one another's lives. They celebrate that I have moved from being a guarded but kind person to someone embracing others in love and grace. I am blessed to have friends spanning the years from grade school, to Auburn, to Houston, to my various work locations, cheering me on as I become who I am meant to be. Recently, one of my teachers from a spiritual direction certification program said that when she first met me, I would share a little bit, but she could see where I still bound myself up to avoid a flood of pain. She knew I needed time to process and reconcile. Now she sees the strength and light radiating from me. This is the mosaic I want others to see.

 Pause and complete Exercise 32.

What are the pieces of your mosaic?

_____

_____

_____

_____

Do you want to add more? What would they be? (Think about characteristics, people, experiences, and so forth.)

_____

_____

_____

_____

_____

> I believe being caught up in the silence, secrecy, and shame of sexual abuse kept women from coming forward to seek healing.

CHAPTER 8
Encouraging Thriving

People were raising their hands claiming
#metoo, but then what? Were they moving into
healing? Were they stuck? Were they holding limiting
beliefs preventing them from living a full life?

Sometimes we are called to do things outside our comfort zones in order to make a difference in the world. We may question our abilities (and maybe even our sanity!) to step out and take action, but when we do, we can have an impact beyond anything we could have ever imagined.

You never know when your passion or purpose will be revealed. You may be off on a career, and then clarity comes and changes your path. I reflected on this because I wondered about my growing passion around two things: the link between sexual abuse and physical health and overcoming the silence and secrecy of sexual abuse. I sensed the need to break the silence and step out to challenge deeply established norms.

 Pause and complete Exercise 33.

You guessed it; moving to thriving wasn't the end of my transformation story. I thought my healing work was done through the therapy and spiritual growth. I had reconciled with my path, felt grounded in my life, and was ready to embrace all the goodness that surrounded me. Then the #metoo movement started in the fall of 2017. I was so proud of the women raising their hands, having the courage to claim their truth. But there was something missing. Something gnawed at me. I would do a daily prayer/meditation in the morning, and I wondered, "What are you saying to me God? What is it that I am sensing?" It took two months for the answer to come. Over breakfast one morning, I was reading an article about the Women's March. One advocate said, "We need more than a march; we need a movement." When I went to prayer after that, it came to me. **These people are raising their hands claiming what happened, but then what? Are they moving? Are they stuck? Are they like I was with my limiting beliefs derailing me, stifling me, preventing me from living my full life?**

I was on fire! I went to my desk to capture all my thoughts: I am a leadership and life coach. I lead retreats—heck, I teach people how to lead retreats. I am a spiritual director. And I have done years of personal work in this space. I can help these people! So I designed a healing retreat to help people who have been through therapy but still find themselves stuck. I see therapy helping people move from victim to survivor, but many things can still hold them back, including harmful mindsets and limiting beliefs. **I believe by looking at these things, shining light on them, and then recasting the thoughts into life-giving ones, people can change the narrative and move to thriving. They can claim a new going-forward story.**

Do you sense something you feel called to do, either for yourself or for others? What would that look like?

Exercise 33

Pause and complete Exercise 34.

I offered this retreat at one of the largest churches in town, a 4,000-person congregation. I knew that about half of the congregants are women and that one-third to one-quarter of women have been sexually abused. These figures are conservative considering how many instances of abuse go unreported. So I should have had at least 500 women who were survivors interested in this opportunity. I wanted to keep it small though, so it would be a safe, sacred space. I was hoping for ten total participants. I had two. My retreat assistant ended up participating because she was a survivor, and it helped the dynamics.

At the end of the retreat, I asked this small group for input: why do they think so few women responded? Maybe because it was at a church and people might feel too public coming to that space? Maybe it needed to be more widely communicated because people must be in a certain place in their lives to take on this kind of growth? So I held my next retreat in a common space, communicated it widely, and had three people interested. Only one person ended up making it to the retreat. Both retreats had incredible things happen,

How does a new "going-forward story" sound to you? Describe it.

Exercise 34

_____

_____

_____

_____

Do you have thoughts or beliefs that get you stuck in unhealthy patterns? Can you name some of them?

_____

_____

_____

_____

and if I could touch any life in a positive way, then it is wonderful. But what was going on?

I believe it was fear. **I believe being caught up in the silence, secrecy, and shame of sexual abuse kept women from coming forward to seek healing.** I started sharing this story by talking about how I wanted to seek justice for the underdog and that my heart hurt for the abused. **In this book, I stand up for "my people," those who have been marginalized and don't feel safe being seen. A hurt and hurting people who can raise their hands with others to say #metoo but don't feel safe enough to step forward for the deeper healing of mind, body, and spirit to claim a full life. I felt convicted to step up for myself and for others by no longer staying small and by sharing my story.**

 Pause and complete Exercise 35.

I have been a facilitator for twenty-five years. I have held retreats for executives and led groups of 500, but the focus was facilitating and not speaking. If you had asked me two years ago, "Tambry, would you stand up in front of a group and share your story?" I would have laughed out loud. That would mean stepping out of my safe box and no longer staying small. That would mean feeling worthy enough to be heard and having a message worth sharing. **The beauty of examining these limiting beliefs is that it frees you up to thrive.** Now here I am, speaking out, telling my story, hoping to encourage others to step forward into the healing.

To me, authenticity means being who we are every moment and in every aspect of our broader lives. When I am at my best, I almost glow and effortlessly shine on others. Yet this can be quickly depleted. The phrase "what would you do if you weren't scared" comes up for me. Fearing criticism, scorn, and judgment held me back from sharing my authentic self. I have defined myself in the past as smart and driven, not open and vulnerable. So the question is, can I find strength, power, love, and joy by stepping out of my comfort zone and into my truth and authentic self? That is what I am seeking to do.

One of my certifications was in the area of diversity. This was life changing because of how much it opened my eyes to various dynamics. It helped me become more comfortable engaging with people who are different from me. **Understanding people's individual truths and experiences is so important. The more I create space for this, the more my world grows.** I believe I was gifted this perspective because I am now being asked to speak at different venues to people with whom I might not be as familiar. For example, when first speaking to university athletes, I had some assumptions around how they might receive me. Yet when I spoke to them, I saw individuals who wanted to hear my story, my pain, my healing, and my hopes for each of them. It is so interesting how so many different aspects of our lives can be used and woven together to make us ready for the next big assignment.

What is also interesting is that I had a dream eight years ago about discussing rape with a group of twenty-somethings. I was trying to get the men to understand the dynamics and also saw some of the women, who were victims, especially of date rape, become emotional and find their voices. When I journaled after the dream, I said, "I don't know what any of this means, but I wonder." I would have never foreseen where my life has taken me. I have had the opportunity to speak on a college campus as well as to groups of women of various ages. My hope is that this book also helps young women understand their emotions and be able to voice their truths.

Does fear hold you back from doing the healing work you need to do? How?

Exercise 35

_____

_____

_____

What does the fear look like?

_____

_____

_____

What does the fear feel like?

_____

_____

_____

_____

Although only a few people attended my retreats, the lives touched made each and every one worth it. One day, a retreat participant gave me a huge compliment. She said, "Tambry, you are so normal." I know, I smiled at that too. But her next statement is where the power is. She said, "It makes me believe I can be normal too." Isn't that what we all want? **Don't we all want to feel normal and live normal, unfettered lives? I want even more than that for others. I want them to live full lives using all of themselves, free from those thoughts, beliefs, past experiences that have been holding them captive for years. I want to help others grow toward the light, allow their truths to permeate the darkness, find the pathways to their souls, and find the hope of peace, joy, love, and healing.**

So here I am sharing my survivor-to-thriver story. I don't want to be known as a victim. My inner little girl doesn't want to be known as a victim. She survived. She survived childhood sexual abuse and the pain of losing so many family members to early deaths. She survived a very abusive first marriage and the on-and-off-again verbal abuse in a second marriage. She survived for forty-five years of her life. But then she moved into thriving. **She was able to look at those things that helped her survive in the past but no longer served her and released them. She knows now how to consciously choose behaviors and mindsets that help her move into her best self and live a full life.**

As I listen to others' stories about their families, I realize there is so much brokenness under the surface. If brokenness and dysfunction exists in all these families, then it could exist for any person around me who is wearing a mask and "putting themselves together" to hide evidence of current or past abuse. I understand this completely, and I lived that way for years. **My hope is that they will see all the life to be lived when you claim your whole self.**

My passion is to help others honestly examine their experiences, pain, and limiting beliefs. We all have found ways to protect ourselves with behaviors and attitudes that help us excel, or at least survive, despite the pain we felt inside. You may have some similar attitudes and strategies, such as staying busy, being "perfect," or proving yourself through your accomplishments. Perhaps you can relate to the sense of "going-away" or "staying small." Are you now seeing that this doesn't always work for you? Are you ready for your awakening moment? Are you ready to do some interior work to reveal what lies beneath the protective shell? Are you ready to remove the layers and unearth your authentic self?

I was encouraged to incorporate more feelings in my writing. Even when I try, I know that it may not come across because of the learned emotional shut down and numbing. This is often a very real, lingering effect of childhood sexual abuse.

I have been increasingly able to touch into the deeper parts of me. In therapy, we would often look at the different "parts" within. Two of my strong parts were my "protector" and my "little girl." Knowing my story, those parts make a lot of sense. The little girl didn't have a voice when things were happening to her, so the protector helped her find ways to survive the abuse, partly by removing her memory of the events. It is important for the little girl to find her voice and claim what she needs, including expressing her anger, rage, and sadness. When I decided to begin sharing my story, I knew I needed to check in with that little girl inside me to see how this would affect her. Would it make her (me) feel too vulnerable? Would it be going too far? When I went inside myself and asked her, listening for her response, I learned that she has a potty mouth. She said, "It will be a 'f--- you!' to him," the man who abused me in my childhood. So there you have it. It is time to stop the secrecy, the silence, and the shame. In finding my voice and my truth, I have found significance in allowing it to encourage others. Are you ready to find yours?

SECTION II

Your Going-Forward Story

As I have taken other women through claiming their going-forward stories, I have been amazed at the transformations. I invite you to walk through the process with me from the comfort of your home. Each step requires reflection and heartfelt work. Go as deep as you want with each step. Consider having a companion journal or notebook to elaborate on your thoughts and insights. Take as much time as seems important. Some people need to spend a good bit of time examining limiting beliefs because they are so ingrained and hard to see. Yet this work is critical because these are the things that underlie your decisions, way of thinking, and sense of self. **Take your time to savor each step of getting to know the essence of you better.**

Hear from other survivors who have been through this process (real names withheld and replaced with flowers):

> **"**Being able to step outside my story and see it objectively was tremendous. The insight about how to bring some change, peace, vision, and practical application to my life offers me the opportunity for less stress, improved communication with others, and clarity to move forward. Thank you, Tambry, for sharing your wisdom and your heart." – Lily

"It has been extremely important in my life to work through the feelings and effects of the trauma I experienced. Yet that chapter of my life feels like it has been on constant auto-replay. This process allowed me the opportunity to begin to move forward into the next chapter of my life. Letting go and moving on does not negate what happened. It will always be a chapter of my life but does not have to be the last chapter. I am now able to see a path into the future and have concrete steps to take to begin to move forward." – Rose

"Being a part of the 'me-too movement' has changed the way I react and feel about flashbacks and memories of 'my incident,' which happened over thirty years ago. But it is as fresh in my mind as if it happened yesterday! Thanks to Tambry, life is now livable. This approach is revolutionary in how it helps a person understand her actions and reactions about her personal experience. It is one-part healing wounds and another part dealing with the anger that comes along with such an assault. Let us not forget the sadness and anger that ensues after one is attacked, groped, or even raped. Tambry helps us get a grip on our feelings, to not let the fear and anger control our very lives or form a barrier between us and all Humanity. Above it all, we can be thrivers in life!" – Iris

"When I heard Tambry's story, I thought, 'I want to feel like her and be confident to overcome the hold my past abuse has on me.' It took courage to begin looking at my story, but I came out feeling powerful. Looking at the bad, grieving the pain, and putting it into perspective has freed me. I didn't know how much lighter I would feel. It has taken until I was sixty to find absolution. No little girl should carry this guilt and pain throughout her life." – Daisy

As you move through this reflection process, I encourage you to have resources available to you. Maybe you have someone with whom you can share your thoughts and realizations. Another idea is to work through this book with another person who wants to seek healing and growth. This would give you a built-in sense of community. Also, as you ponder on the chapters of your story, if you find you need to go back and do some trauma work, have a trusted therapist you can engage. For me, having someone with a background in internal family systems and somatic healing was valuable. Working through the layers of muck that have built up over the years may bring up new pieces to explore. Please know that this is not going backward—you are still growing, expanding, and excavating your beautiful, authentic self.

Resources are also available at survivorstothrivers.com, including suggested readings, ideas around physical activities, and the bimonthly blog that gives helpful insights and healing exercises. You can also contact me through the website with questions, thoughts, and insights.

"
What this means
is that we have to
'unfreeze' ourselves
from the protective
layers that have
formed in order to
get to the real, core
part of ourselves.

"

CHAPTER 9
Welcoming Change

I no longer wanted to listen to the negative inner
voice that sought to destroy my God-given potential.

As we examine our lives, we are given the opportunity to ask, "How's it working for you?" If the answer is that you are not where you hoped to be or you find yourselves repeating the same unhelpful patterns, maybe it is time to write a new chapter.

Abraham Maslow called reaching your full potential "self-actualization" (Maslow, 1943). As a psychology graduate student, I thought it was a nice concept but really wondered if we can rise above the demands of daily life and inscribed instincts and behaviors to reach that level of living. Several decades since that thought, I have realized that it is a journey, one that requires shedding away those things we have built up to protect ourselves at an instinctual level to survive. These are boundaries we encounter or create that inhibit us from achieving our greatest potential. Two metaphors around this transformation come to mind for me. One is that of refining gold. This process involves melting away all that isn't pure to be left, ultimately, with what is precious. The other metaphor is that of a sculptor chipping away at all that is not meant to be in the final creation. I feel like I have been through both processes at different times of my life.

 Pause and complete Exercise 36.

In a world of Facebook posts showing the wonderful places we see, the multitude of friends we enjoy, the incredible lives we live, it is nice to see when someone shares the less-than-perfect, less-wonderful side. We can feel inadequate if we compare our real, daily lives to some of the carefully crafted images on social media. I know I have put up an image of having it all together, creating walls that kept me protected but also kept people from getting close. I have told you about the very refined professional persona I constructed, even subconsciously. In my growth, I have realized that those walls kept me from what I want: meaningful relationships, meaningful work, and a meaningful life. My vulnerability encourages others around me to do the same. That is when we can be truly present for each other, in good times and bad.

This is important to consider when we think about the nature of change. In our lives, we all consciously and unconsciously build structures around ourselves that help us feel safe and secure. The problem is that as we grow and evolve, those structures can change from helpful to binding. In the book *The Untethered Soul: The Journey Beyond Yourself* (2007), Michael Singer talks about how we can build an environment around us that is quite comfortable, fully climate controlled, and predictable. Yet when you go outside those walls you created, you see the abundance of natural light and the flow of life you have been missing. The way to move and shift to embrace the world around you is to no longer support, maintain, or defend your fortress. Instead, allow your mind, body, and soul to

Does an analogy come up for you when you think about the process of self-actualization? How does it illustrate your sense of this or your desire?

Exercise 36

_____

_____

_____

_____

_____

_____

_____

_____

_____

move into the beauty and light that has always been there. You can do this slowly to allow yourself to adjust, just like when you step into the light after being awhile in a dark space and it takes time for your eyes to adjust.

Another book called *Open the Door: A Journey to the True Self* (2008) by Joyce Rupp was very helpful for me as I sought to open myself up to possibilities. It uses the door of your heart as a metaphor to be examined. As I worked through that image, I saw that my door opened outward and that I could go through when I was ready. And I was more than ready. I was excited and had a sense that goodness awaited me. The sun was bright and warm. The flowers were colorful, cheerful, and brilliant. It was a new, beautiful season for me. As I walked forward, I knew it was a safe space God created for me. It was a place that I could feel God's love and just be. It was like I was leaving the box in which I had been contained and could grow into a new, open space. Outside the door, I could see where I could flourish. The message that hung on the door was "please enter," inviting me to enter the new space that awaited me.

 Pause and complete Exercise 37.

As we think about moving through that door and accepting the invitation, we know it will require movement and change. Many books have been written about change management. Although these are usually written for a corporate setting, I believe they hold much that individuals can learn as we seek changes in our lives. The first basic principle is that you have to become dissatisfied with the current state to be able to move into a new way of being. The familiarity and comfort of what you know and have become accustomed to must be examined. That brings us back to the question, "How is it working for you?" This is a time for you to be honest with yourself. You can even practice listening to your body as you ask that question. As you think about the notes you took during the first section of the book, how are you feeling about your current state? (You can take time now to go back and review your comments and thoughts.) Are you living the life you want to live?

 Pause and complete Exercise 38.

Can you reflect on the door of your heart?
What does it look like?

Do you have a sense of the space that is beyond the door?

What invitation do you see? What message hangs on the door?

What reflections would you like to pull forward from the first section of the book to serve as reminders of your perspective on your current story?

_____

_____

_____

_____

_____

_____

_____

_____

How do you feel about your current chapter?
What thoughts come with the idea of shifting into a new one?

_____

_____

_____

_____

_____

_____

_____

_____

_____

Some change management theories talk about "unfreeze – change – refreeze."[1] What this means is that we have to "unfreeze" ourselves from the protective layers that have formed in order to get to the real, core part of ourselves. After the unfreezing, you can build upon the ground that has been thawed. Seeing this as the natural process of melting ice might be a gentler image than the "chipping away" I mentioned earlier. If you have been in a climate with snow, you have seen how the early spring flowers begin blooming as the ice and snow melt away. Movement and expansion are possible then.

Another important piece of change is having a line of sight to your destination. You need to feel safe and confident as you shift to a new way of being. That is what section II of the book is all about. I will guide you as you begin to envision your going-forward story. Together, we will explore the "main character" of your story and perhaps examine yourself in ways you have never seen. Give yourself permission to be curious and capture insights that come up for you. Don't filter insights. These are gifts you are giving yourself. Like my story, some of the insights may not make sense initially, but as you continue to explore, their meaning may become evident. Think about it as untangling a delicate necklace; allow the beauty to unfold before you.

 Pause and complete Exercise 39.

I feel that Brené Brown has helped the world greatly with her research around vulnerability. Her book, *Daring Greatly: How the Courage to Be Vulnerable Transforms the Way We Live, Love, Parent, and Lead* (2012), was instrumental as I learned how to feel my way through experiences and emotions. She encourages us to engage in what she calls "wholehearted living" where we can feel a sense of worthiness, love, and belonging. She says that vulnerability is the birthplace of joy, creativity, and love. That is what I am asking of you: to be vulnerable, even if it is just to yourself. As survivors, being vulnerable is everything we have built our walls up to avoid. We think that being vulnerable can lead to being a victim, and there is no way we want to go back there. That is why I wanted to share my story first before I asked this of you. You can see that my vulnerability allowed me to slowly and safely examine those walls, see my strength within them, and know that I no longer needed to wall off from the shadows.

---

1   Kurt Lewin's change management model developed in the 1940s is credited with the beginning of this thought and theory.

What large changes have you been through in your life?

What helped you move through the changes?

What do you wish you had done?

What do you want to give yourself permission to do?

Oprah Winfrey and Deepak Chopra frequently hold virtual meditation series. One of those series was called *"Getting Unstuck: Creating a Limitless Life"* (The Chopra Center, 2013), where they discussed the fact that we are conditioned by old habits, memories, wounds, and beliefs, but by seeing ourselves with clarity in the present moment, we can stand apart from automatic responses and tap into the highest expression of self. This aligns with my realization that I didn't want to listen to the negative inner voice that sought to destroy my God-given potential. Instead, I sought to become the best version of myself and play from my heart again. Together, we are going to gently look at some of those old wounds and beliefs, so you will be able to claim and release them. In doing so, you will be getting yourself "unstuck" in order to move into the highest expression of you.

In *Healing the Wounded Heart: The Heartache of Sexual Abuse and the Hope of Transformation* (2016), Dan B. Allender says we often find it easier to shrug off what has hurt us rather than stepping into what feels overwhelming to engage. In other words, we would rather stay in that stuck and "frozen" place because it feels familiar. But remember that sexual harm, like all hurt and brokenness, doesn't fade away just because we minimize it, numb it, or try to forget it. While the price to name our abuse and hurt may be high, it is far higher if we refuse to do so. We can reclaim only what we name. If we refuse to enter our past with honesty, sensitivity, and wisdom, the harm of the past will continue to wage war against us in the present. We must bravely step into that bold new space of fully living.

I have shared insights from thought leaders to encourage you as we take steps to shift you from your current state into what is possible for you. In other words, these are all the reasons I ask you to join me in this journey of healing and hope.

 Pause and complete Exercise 40.

What authors or thought leaders have encouraged you? This could be books you've read, talks you have heard, or concepts you have pondered.

_____

_____

_____

_____

_____

_____

What insights do you want to capture now?

_____

_____

_____

_____

_____

_____

"

Looking at your
actions and patterns
can be insightful and,
yes, scary. At least
it was for me. Part
of that examination
is looking at the
whole of you.

"

CHAPTER 10
Honoring Your Whole Self

*I had separated my head from my body with a
thick stone wall. I barely recognized that
I had physical and emotional feelings below.*

Did you know that the word "heal" comes from the word "whole"? That is why it is so important to consider your whole self—mind, body, and spirit. Since all aspects of us are interdependent, we can't just take an isolated look to heal one part. We often try to numb ourselves to deny that there may be any pain physically or emotionally. Sadly, suppressing these messages can just lead to depression and/or anxiety, which can lead to other unhealthy behaviors. It was a powerful connection to my past experiences and thinking when I heard the saying, "Depression is anger turned inward." I would feel depressed and see that as weakness, something I needed to suppress because I needed to be capable and strong. It took a long time for me to realize that not looking at it just kept it in the dark; it didn't make it go away. The courageous thing is to shine the light in and see what is going on under the surface.

 Pause and complete Exercise 41.

Looking at your actions and patterns can be insightful and, yes, scary. At least it was for me. Part of that examination is looking at the whole of you. For me, I lived in my head and didn't really recognize that I had a body, much less a spirit. I felt safer in my head. Unfortunately, "the mind may forget, but the body always remembers." I reflect on this wisdom I shared earlier from my therapist because it speaks a helpful truth, particularly as we seek to honor our whole selves.

What resonates for you when you hear about embracing "mind, body, and spirit?"

_____

_____

_____

_____

_____

What has your experience been with examining and honoring all three aspects?

_____

_____

_____

_____

_____

_____

What intention do you wish to set as you move into examining your story?

_____

_____

_____

_____

_____

_____

I was recently reminded of this. One of the rights of passage as you move into your fifties is experiencing the fun of a colonoscopy. Yay me! Dear friends gave me tips to move through the prep and procedure as easily as possible. I went into the hospital for the procedure with the attitude that it was a standard procedure and I would be just fine. When the nurse stuck the IV into my arm, she had a hard time finding a vein, and I yelped in pain as the needle went in. I continued to hurt as she taped things down but tried to control my whimpers. Then the overwhelming tears came. All of a sudden, the physical pain was tied to past emotional pain. I reflected on what could be behind it. Suddenly, it came to me. The last time I was in this situation (on a gurney with an IV) was six years prior when my ex-husband told me he was leaving me but would be there for me through the shoulder surgery. His announcement had come out of nowhere, with no previous discussions. As I was wheeled back to the operating room, I was sobbing feeling abandoned during the first time I ever really needed him. The person wheeling me assured me things would be fine with the procedure. What she didn't understand was the tears were about what was going to happen after the surgery.

So there I was, alone in a hospital room being stuck with a painful IV, and the suppressed memories flooded back. The blessing is that I had done the work to know that I am worthy of love and care. I knew that I would not be abandoned by those who love me and surround me now. The nurse went and found my dear, kind husband who came back to console me. I knew this time and this person were entirely different, but emotions aren't always rational.

This is such a simple example of how "the body keeps the score" (Van der Kolk, 2014). My body stored my memories even when I sought to move on into a happy marriage. I had not thought about having PTSD (post-traumatic stress disorder) from that surgery episode six years ago, but it does make sense. The experience tapped into my worst childhood fears (not being cared for or worthy), and I went through two incredibly hard years starting at that point. To be able to slow down and acknowledge the connection and insight was incredibly healing, which is what I hope for you as you go through the exercises I give you. They are opportunities for you to explore and gain insights around aspects of your story.

 Pause and complete Exercise 42.

Opening my mind to these concepts has taken years, and I had to experience these insights to believe their credibility. Years ago, my therapist knew I had

In chapter 5, I asked you to reflect on times your body has spoken to you. Having read about this experience, do additional examples come up for you when your body led you to deeper insight around an event?

Exercise 42

_____

_____

_____

_____

_____

Is there more learning you would like to capture?

_____

_____

_____

_____

_____

How have previous experiences by you or others helped to bring insight?

_____

_____

_____

_____

_____

_____

_____

more physical healing to do. The pain in my joints was almost unbearable at times. She introduced me to a doctor from China whom many people would go to when Western medicine failed. This doctor would use reflexology only on my feet to diagnose and treat my whole-body symptoms. This experience expanded my understanding of how the body is so interconnected.

Since this was early in my healing journey, I had to overcome much skepticism. I wish I had been even more open to what the doctor had to teach me. For example, I laughed it off when he told me my ailments were related to pent-up stress, and in broken English he said, "What you so worried about?" My internal response was, "You have no idea!" because the worry was based on the ramifications of the sexual abuse. Yet maybe he could sense this truth, and if I had engaged him more readily, he may have been a greater source of light into my darkness. I share this because I want you to be open to the various resources that surround you, some of which you may initially discount. One phrase I often use with my clients is "be curious," and I offer it to you. Be curious and be open to multiple avenues for your healing.

One thing I wondered about was my body's experience with yoga. For years, I was not able to do it because of the cramps in my feet and pain in my joints, especially my knees. After my shoulder surgery, I began seeing a massage therapist to help with recovery. He said the type of pent-up pain I felt during yoga was not uncommon and that he could help me release it, so I could ultimately do yoga without hurting. As I worked with him to address the pain, we found it going into my shins, so he identified and worked on my trigger points. Later, he told me that my body would have recruited all those muscles to fight. That is why it hurt so much for me to jog and to lay on my back, because all those muscles were so tight. The muscle memory held them tight and created the tension and pain. I was fascinated that the cause of my body's tightness might be from past trauma. As I read more, I learned that yoga is one of the things recommended for people recovering from trauma, particularly sexual abuse. When I made these connections with my experience, I had a sense that it would help me understand and empathize with others in the future.

At the time, I didn't know all the ways God would use this intense time of healing. My ex-husband was out of the picture, which freed me to do what was necessary to heal. This therapist not only helped with my arm recovery, but also helped release tension stored in my body from the trauma all those years ago. Once again, the doors were opened, and I was walking through them. I would not have known the doors even existed in the past, but I continued trying to listen to God's cues. I was amazed at how the integration happened—mind, body, and spirit. I may not have believed it if I hadn't experienced it. I invite you to enjoy this season of rebirth and release the ties that bind.

 Pause and complete Exercise 43.

Understanding the body connection is important as you move into exploring your story. I had to learn to trust my body when I doubted myself and my memories. Many survivors find themselves in disbelief asking, "Am I making it all up? Did it happen? What is the reality?" The dark story begins unfolding underneath the sterile mask that was created to protect or survive. I can assure you, my body told me loudly to believe the dark story. My therapist said a part of me was still trying to protect me from the truth, the truth that was too painful to handle as a child. That was why I couldn't tap into the memories for years. Many memories are still locked away. The realizations that did come forward would, at times, cause nausea and dizziness. Other times, tension would build up in my core, through my body, and I felt like I might explode. Then I would feel tired, exhausted, and desperate for sleep.

All of this may sound terrible. But I suspect you have already experienced it or something like it. To look it in the face and take its power away is where you will find your strength and claim your going-forward story. Now I can see situations for what they truly are and recognize my triggered reactions. I can create space, which is healthy, and ask for what I need. Triggers and reactions will always be there, but claiming the space helps me choose my response. Removing this layer of reaction allows me to tap into the deeper reality driving the triggers. I can see them for what they are, just like when I reacted to getting the IV before the colonoscopy.

At times, we trap the pain we experience inside us to protect ourselves and feel strong. Shedding tears might feel vulnerable, so we stuff them down so deeply that we may not even recognize them. We build our walls so as to not be hurt by others, but that further solidifies the pain within those walls, within us. We need to allow the pain to pass through us and out, not gird ourselves against it. Allowing pain and even fear to flow through us, to experience and then release it, takes its power away.

But if you don't know what the pain or fear is and the dimensions of it, how can you release it? Journaling around this can be very helpful. Writing down the pain and or fear you are experiencing is the first step. Acknowledge that it is

Do you have parts of your body that are painful or tense? Where are they?

_____

_____

_____

_____

_____

If you don't immediately know, take a deep breath and do a "body scan." Notice whether there is tension, resistance, or pain as you move down from the top of your head to your toes. As you encounter any tension or pain, breathe into that space. What do you notice?

_____

_____

_____

_____

_____

_____

Write about any resistance, pain, or tension you may have noticed and what it's trying to protect you from.

_____

_____

_____

_____

there. That alone may be enough to take its power away, because when you shine light on it, you can see it for what it truly is. Don't allow it to lurk in the darkness and shadows. If you need to take this a step further, wonder about the pain and fear. Ask it: "Where do you come from? What do I need to know about you?" Check in with your body and see if you feel physical pain or tightness. Can you breathe into that space and release a little?

A finite amount of energy lies within us, and as we hold pain inside or strive to keep it at arm's length, we are expending that energy. By allowing the pain to flow through us, we have more energy to do other things. Doing this helped me step out of denial, through pain, and into acceptance.

 Pause and complete Exercise 44.

What is your sense of this concept? What comes to mind when you think of holding pain and fear inside? Exercise 44

_____

_____

_____

_____

What would you do with the extra energy available to you if you let go of pain and fear?

_____

_____

_____

_____

_____

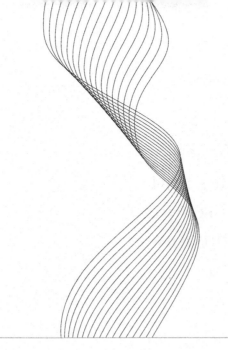

This examination could be a completely "head" or thinking activity, although I encourage you to use all of yourself (mind, body, and spirit) as you work through this section. **Take time to pause and see if your body or spirit want you to add to what your mind had you write.** As you pause, a way to help get into a "mindful place" is by taking three deep breaths. Breathe in slowly allowing air to fill your lungs and then breathe out just as slowly. Sit and notice how your body feels after just that level of intentionality. A way to keep this mindset in place is to light a candle as you write or journal. The flame can represent spirit for you. I will put this reminder out periodically to encourage you to engage your "whole self."

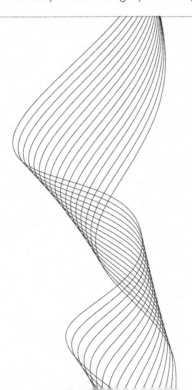

"

Core beliefs are
tied to attitudes and
thoughts that result
in certain behaviors
and actions.

"

CHAPTER 11
Examining the Core of You

*Slowing down to listen to your internal "knowing"
is critical. Taking in all the presented facts,
instead of just the ones that fit your pattern,
will help you make critical changes.*

~~~~~~~~~~~~~~~~~~

The first step is to understand the "main character" of your story, which is you. We will capture the basic facts and the essence of you, including your limiting beliefs. This entails looking at patterns that can keep you in a loop of heartache and hopelessness if unresolved. Capturing where you are now is the first step in change because it helps you assess the current state. By objectively seeing this, you begin to understand what you want to be different to motivate you to do the "unfreezing," letting go, going beyond past limitations and boundaries.

This starts with exploring various aspects of you, in other words, looking at the core of who you are. You have innate aspects and characteristics, such as your personality, and learned aspects, such as core beliefs and values.

Let's begin with the innate aspects and characteristics. Think of a "character sketch" you would do if writing a book or movie script. Reminder: if you want to have an additional journal to capture your thoughts, that will allow you to be more expansive in your reflections.

 Pause and complete Exercises 45 and 46.

The Main Character

Reflect on the main character. What are the basic facts (age, gender, ethnicity, family makeup, and so forth)?

What are the main interests and activities?

What was childhood like? (For example, think about strongest memory, influencers, proudest moments, wounds—the kind of things I shared in chapter 2.)

_____
_____
_____
_____
_____
_____
_____
_____
_____
_____
_____
_____
_____
_____
_____
_____
_____
_____
_____
_____
_____

Think about the main character's strengths and gifts. These may be things you have discovered about yourself or things others have told you. Many times, we are not even aware of our strengths because they come naturally and we assume everyone has them. If you are working through this book with another person, this would be a nice time for them to share the strengths and gifts they see in you and vice versa. Asking others for this insight is always valuable and interesting. When I do client coaching, one tool we often use is called 360-degree feedback. That means that you ask people around you from all angles to share their perspective about you. Consider asking important people in your life what they see in you.

 Pause and complete Exercise 47.

It is also helpful to look at what roles you play in your life. Some of these roles might be every day, and others may be less frequent but still very important. In the left-hand column, list the roles that come to mind. After you have captured them, move to the right-hand column and order these roles considering level of importance. Does this comparison bring any insight to you? What is it?

List the main character's strengths and gifts. Exercise 47

Pause and complete Exercise 48.

Dreams or Desires Held

With this next section, give yourself time to contemplate what dreams you have for your life. Many of us don't allow ourselves this freedom. Sometimes

1. List your roles. 2. Rank them in order of importance.   Exercise 48

_____

_____

_____

_____

What do you notice about the comparison?

_____

_____

_____

_____

Is there anything about this exercise of listing and ordering your roles that you want to capture?

_____

_____

_____

_____

_____

it is because no one has ever asked, and other times it may be a way to guard ourselves and avoid disappointment. If nothing comes up for you right away, feel free to come back to this section.

Pause and complete Exercise 49.

Describe your greatest dream. Exercise 49

_____

_____

_____

_____

_____

What do you deeply want?

_____

_____

_____

_____

_____

What do you really need?

_____

_____

_____

_____

_____

I have expressed how important looking at mind, body and spirit has been to me in my healing and claiming my whole self. These words and concepts can be powerful expressions of who we are and how we want to grow. Take some time to describe and define each for yourself.

Pause and complete Exercise 50.

Describe what each means to you: Exercise 50

Mind

_____

_____

_____

_____

Body

_____

_____

_____

_____

Spirit

_____

_____

_____

_____

Now consider how much attention you give to each part. An easy way to do this is to think of dividing up a pie into three pieces. How much of that pie do you give to activities that nurture your mind? How about your body? Your spirit? After you complete the first circle, consider an ideal world. In your desired going-forward world, how much of that pie would you want to give to each piece? **How would you divide up your mind-body-spirit pie?** *(Write what falls into each.)*

 Pause and complete Exercise 51.

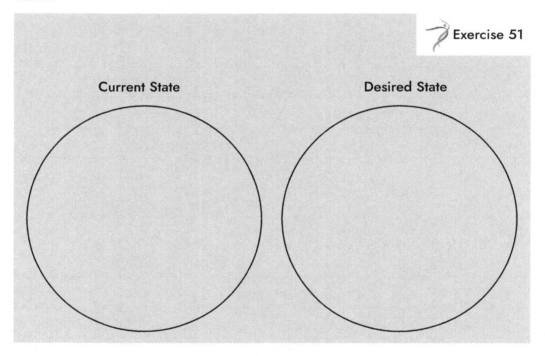

Exercise 51

Current State

Desired State

Core Beliefs

Next, let's examine core beliefs or values, the long-standing views that we hold about ourselves, other people, and the world in which we live, work, and play. They define how we believe things operate and influence what we do and how we engage. They serve as filters or guides to help us make sense of the world. Core beliefs are developed over time based on interaction with family, friends, community, media, and other experiences. Because they have been expressed around us for so long, we often are not able to even recognize that they exist. We need to bring them into the light, into our awareness, because they are not always accurate or helpful. Core beliefs are tied to attitudes and thoughts that result in certain behaviors and actions.

Here is an example of how a core belief can influence decisions and interactions. I have shared how I always tried to be a "good girl." This meant that I tried to follow the rules. Imagine me driving down a road and coming upon a "left lane ends, merge right" sign. Well, of course I follow the rules and merge. The right lane begins to back up with all the other people who are following the sign's direction. Next a car comes racing down the left lane passing all the cars that obediently followed the sign a half mile back. My core belief then turns into a thought and attitude of, "I can't believe that they didn't merge. Do they think they are above the rules?" This then leads me to the action and behavior of getting closer to the car in front of me so that no one can "break in line." This is not the most favorable description of myself, but I am sure you have seen it happen or maybe have even done it yourself.

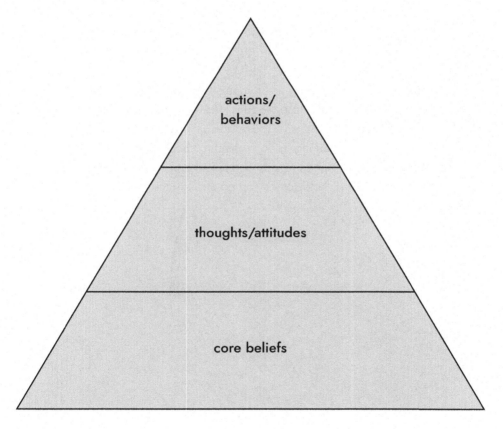

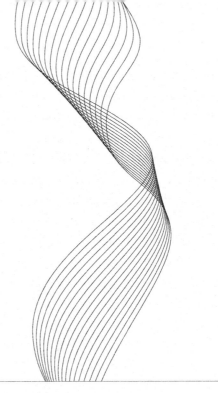

How are you doing using all of yourself (mind, body, and spirit) as you work through these sections? Are you **pausing** to see if your body or spirit wants you to add to what your mind had you write? Are you **breathing** as you reflect to check in on your inner knowing? Do you need to stop and take the three deep breaths again? Use your whole self as you go through the next exercise.

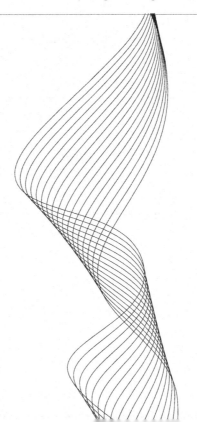

The work is to think about what core beliefs are strong for you and how they drive your behavior. Look particularly at those core beliefs that don't lead you to be the person you want to be. I want to be a gracious and kind person, but you wouldn't see that in my actions as I nudged out the line breaker in the merging lane.

We form these core beliefs around a number of topics or areas. I have listed a few below to get you thinking. The categories alone are neutral. Rather, the mindset around them can lead a core belief to be limiting.

The first core belief listed is "achievement." I have told you that achievement was a big driver and motivator for me. Unfortunately, it led to some less helpful attitudes that included letting it define who I was as well as allowing it to impact relationships. I invite you to circle five core beliefs that are foundational to you, ones that create the bedrock of who you are. You can also write in your own as this certainly is not a comprehensive list.

 Pause and complete Exercise 52.

Sample List of Core Beliefs			Exercise 52
Achievement	Excellence	Independence	Personal Growth
Beauty	Faithfulness	Integrity	Power
Collaboration	Family	Joy	Productivity
Communication	Forgiveness	Learning	Purpose
Community	Freedom	Love	Quality
Compassion	Frugality	Loyalty	Respect
Competence	Fulfillment	Money	Risk Taking
Competition	Fun	Nurturing	Success
Creativity	Genuineness	Obedience	Tolerance
Determination	Hard Work	Orderliness	Tranquility
Discipline	Honesty	Peace	Trust
Efficiency	Humor	Perfection	Truth

To help you begin to expand your understanding of the core beliefs that you hold deeply, reflect on the messages that you heard in your childhood. They may have been said directly or inferred, or your child-mind may have made them up to explain your experiences. Some of mine were: *always* be above reproach, be there for others, stay small, and don't stand out; *never* be lazy, idle, or rely on anyone; and *I must* be concerned for others above myself, protect others, and have it all together.

Pause and complete Exercise 53.

What statements follow the words below for you?

Exercise 53

Always . . .

_____

_____

_____

_____

_____

_____

_____

Never . . .

_____

_____

_____

_____

_____

_____

_____

_____

I must . . .

_____

_____

_____

_____

_____

As you look at these thoughts and phrases, begin to evaluate them.
What is the source for these core beliefs? What are the facts? What is true?
Do the beliefs serve you? How or how not?

_____

_____

_____

_____

_____

_____

_____

_____

_____

_____

_____

_____

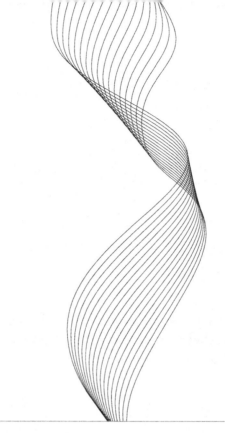

How are you doing using all of yourself (mind, body, and spirit) as you work through these sections? Are you **pausing** to see if your body or spirit wants you to add to what your mind had you write? Are you **breathing** as you reflect to check in on your inner knowing? Is your candle still lit?

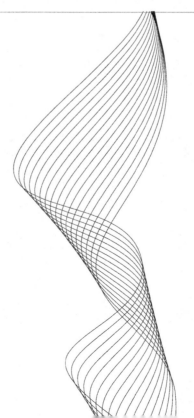

Here is where the interesting work really begins. As you look at some of those core beliefs and messages, identify which ones are not true or are not helpful. Let's examine them. Just as I did with the car line example, look at that core belief and identify what thoughts or attitudes come up, as well as the resulting actions or behaviors. Here is an example for one of my core beliefs that I have talked about throughout the book. It follows the format of the pyramid I shared with you earlier in the chapter.

		Negative/Unhelpful	Positive/Helpful
STEP 3	Action/Behavior	Striving for grades, achievements, and accolades to prove myself and gain love.	
STEP 2	Thought/Attitude	I must prove my worth, earn my value.	
STEP 1	Core Belief	I am not worthy.	

Taking a step forward with this activity, now look at what can happen if you shift that core belief to a positive and see how it plays out in how you see yourself. As you look at my example, the action I take, "striving for grades and achievements," is not negative on the surface and can be admirable, but what is driving that effort is not healthy. I will always strive to do my best, but now I can also rest in the fact that I am inherently worthy. So as I shift my thinking around my core belief to "I am worthy," see how it feeds up through the pyramid to my thoughts and attitudes and finally my actions and behaviors.

		Negative/Unhelpful	Positive/Helpful
STEP 3	Action/Behavior	Striving for grades, achievements, and accolades to prove myself and gain love.	I can be my true self to be loved and valued. My actions are authentic.
STEP 2	Thought/Attitude	I must prove my worth, earn my value.	I have inherent value in who I am.
STEP 1	Core Belief	I am not worthy.	I am worthy.

Now it is your turn. Pick out a core belief that you believe gets in the way of your best living and most-fruitful life. Start with the negative column and write in the core belief, then the resulting thought/attitude, and finally the action/behavior. After you have done that, restate the core belief in a positive frame. Reflect on what the following thought and attitude would be. Then move to describe what the corresponding action and behavior could look like. After you fill out this matrix, you can practice with other core beliefs in your journal using the model below.

Pause and complete Exercise 54.

Exercise 54

		Negative/Unhelpful	Positive/Helpful
STEP 3	Action/Behavior		
STEP 2	Thought/Attitude		
STEP 1	Core Belief		

Since our minds cannot handle infinite possibilities, we create our own realities with finite thoughts. Unconsciously, we take the whole realm of possibilities, break it into pieces, and select a handful of pieces to put together in a certain way within our minds. This "mental model" becomes our reality. We expend energy day and night to make the world fit this model, and label everything that doesn't fit as wrong, bad, or unfair. If we want to go beyond the model that we have created, we have to take the risk of questioning it, no longer believing in it.

As you begin to question and even stop doing some of the things that have become automatic and comfortable for you, you will experience some discomfort. Become curious as to why that is. Yes, I am encouraging you to step out of your comfort zone. As you step out into the unknown, you will begin to see the walls that you have built and the limits you have put on yourself. Seeing this will begin to reveal the repetitive loop of behaviors and thinking that lead you into a pattern of living from the unresolved hurt of the past.

Pause and complete Exercise 55.

What do you know about your mental models and comfort zones?

Exercise 55

Limiting Beliefs

These unhelpful patterns or limiting beliefs are tricky because they are so embedded that you may not even see them. Unconsciously, my limiting belief of not being worthy led to striving to prove myself through achieving high grades, positions, and certifications. This seems benign enough. But there is a dangerous aspect to it when limiting beliefs influence your decision-making. As "smart" as I was as I entered the University of Houston's doctoral program, I was very "dumb" about whom I entered it with. I shared earlier about the guy I dated from my sophomore to senior year in college. His confidence and charisma seemed to compliment what I considered to be my weaker side. There were signs of abusiveness, but the familiar "I am unworthy" mantra that played in my mind drowned out the voice of truth I needed to hear. Once married and in Houston, the abuse increased with verbal attacks, threats, and mind manipulation. I would tell myself that he wasn't beating me, so it could have been worse, once again downplaying what was happening. My body began to tell me that it wasn't OK. **Slowing down to listen to your internal "knowing" is critical. Taking in all the presenting facts instead of just the ones that fit your pattern will help you make critical changes.** I had to remove myself from that situation to see how toxic it truly was.

The good news is that I was taking a step to claim my worthiness and what was right for me. Eventually, I also determined that I really didn't need a doctorate to do what I wanted to do, so I began to change the pattern of having to be "the best" and using achievements to define me. The bad news is that my limiting beliefs were deeply ingrained, and I could still fall into thinking that if I was best in my class, if I mastered the certifications, if I earned the next degree, then that proved I was worthy. These things helped me feel invincible to any hurtful experiences that might come at me. Sadly, this invincible wall also kept out desired things as well, like loving relationships.

Limiting mindsets can show up in other, less dramatic ways, in the workplace for example. If you had asked me whether I was a trusting person, I would have said yes. But in reality, I only trusted with the easy things. Being vulnerable, which required a great amount of trust, was and is very difficult. But I loved being there for others and having others trust me.

I remember an Outward Bound trip with a senior leadership team. I was part of the team as an organizational development consultant. The senior leader was passionate about the trip. Partly due to my role and partly my personality, I felt a responsibility for this experience to go well even though I wasn't in charge.

Our lead guide decided to scale a rock face even though it was freezing and rainy. When we got the team to the top of the mountain, I was aware that one woman was pale and shaking. I immediately got the guide's attention, and we had everyone surround her to increase her body temperature. Next, we had to get everyone back down the mountain, and one man was terrified. I got beside him and said, "We are going down together." Side by side, we rappelled down the rock face with me encouraging this man who was twice my size.

When I got to the ledge where one of the guides was standing, she asked, "Are you OK?" That was when I crumbled. I was grateful for her seeing me and showing concern about my well-being. My pattern has been to be there for everyone else and put my needs at the bottom. I found significance by being there for others, but I couldn't be "needy" myself. In this moment of being the object of the caring outreach, my heart was touched.

I have learned through self-reflection that I adopted self-sufficiency at a young age. No one asked me, "Are you OK?" Everyone around me was living their own traumas, so I learned that in order to not be disappointed, I needed to take care of myself. What I didn't know and had to learn later is that relationships are built by leaning on one another and being vulnerable to one another. The guide and others around me were challenging and gently dismantling my wall of self-reliance. Maybe the world and my life would work better if I didn't just try to be there for everyone around me but actually allowed others to be there for me.

Another example comes from my diversity practitioner training. We learned a feedback model (Riley, 1999) that stated three steps: (1) specifically share what the other person has done to hurt or offend you, (2) state the impact on you, and (3) name what you need in the future from that person. We had to do this real time with someone in our group who had done something to offend us during our months together. My person and example came to mind quickly. It took a moment, but ultimately, I was able to name the impact it had on me. What stopped me in my tracks was stating what I needed in the future. I don't know how I looked to the others around me, but in my mind, I was the wide-eyed emoji, a deer in the headlights. I truly can't remember if I was able to name what I needed in that moment. This is how hard pattern breaking can be. **The recognition that something needs to be addressed and then the ability to reprogram ourselves to think and be different is difficult, yet it is the core of self-actualization.**

Now, it is time to look more deeply at the limiting beliefs that have developed in you. What vulnerabilities exist given your personality, core beliefs, or life experiences? What are the tender areas where you are especially sensitive to criticism, rejection, and failure? These limiting beliefs can serve as triggers that plunge us into old scripts about how we are defective in some way. We need to look at them because they get in the way of us being our best selves.

 Pause and complete Exercise 56.

With self-awareness comes the willingness to be honest with yourself and others. My perfectionist wall was built so that I couldn't be criticized or hurt. I would review things multiple times to make sure they were accurate and complete. I wanted to catch errors before anyone else. I wanted to impress so that I would be worthy of whatever position I held. These are the kinds of things that led me to receive the "professional" feedback. When I was told that I needed to be less polished and more real to take my performance to the next level, I didn't understand what that meant. I didn't realize what was missing was the relational piece. I wasn't giving people the personal side of me. What I know after much self-reflection is that it didn't feel safe. This ties back to my difficulty around being vulnerable. I had learned to lean on IQ and perfection because they were bulletproof. But that meant entering every situation as if I were engaging in war and not partnership. In business, sadly, sometimes that is required, but the key is slowing down to assess the situation and determine what response options are available and which one is the most appropriate.

I teach a course on leading retreats. I have led offsites and retreats for over twenty years and still review my notes before class because I want to make sure I cover all my material. Yet what I have found is that some of the best learning moments happen serendipitously when I make a mistake and name it. Using my humanity and vulnerability helps my students see themselves in me even more than when I cover the material perfectly. I also find that I have more fun that way.

Let's look more deeply at the limiting beliefs that seek to protect our vulnerability. I call it "looking into the dark." This is our way of shining light into areas that have existed for years but now need to be examined. I have heard it said that it is important to "look back without staring." To me, that means looking back to recognize what is important to know and understand but not get mired down in the bitterness and resentment that can come. It is about recognizing and overcoming voices and tendencies that have developed so that you can move forward. Be curious as you explore the questions below. Consider yourself dialoguing with the limiting belief.

What internal obstacles or limiting beliefs get in the way of your best self? (They may have developed over time, may be core beliefs that formed when you were young, or could be based on life experiences.)

How do they show up?

How do they keep you from your best self?

Pause and complete Exercise 57.

Name the limiting belief:

Now ask, where do you come from? What are you trying to protect?

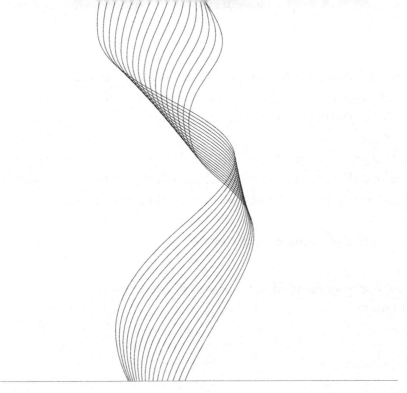

Limiting beliefs can be difficult. Are you still **pausing** to see if your body or spirit wants you to add to what your mind had you write? Are you **breathing** as you reflect to check in on your inner knowing?

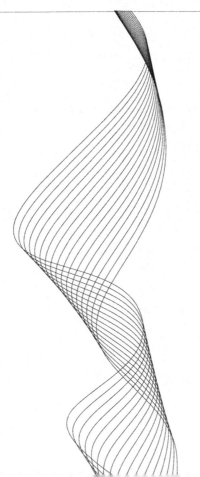

In your journal or notebook, you can continue to answer these questions for other limiting beliefs that you have identified. It may also be helpful to take a break in between the limiting belief explorations if you have multiple ones you wish to examine.

Take yourself one more step into the dark as you seek to acknowledge, claim, and then heal those tender spots that have developed over time. They may have served you well in the past, but now they need to be released.

Pause and complete Exercise 58.

What pain or wounds need to be healed to overcome these barriers?

Exercise 58

_____

_____

_____

_____

_____

_____

What would your healing prayer or healing intention be?

_____

_____

_____

_____

_____

_____

_____

We all have been wounded to some degree. What we do with the woundedness defines us. If we learn and grow from it, it can be a catalyst. If we bind it, never allowing it air to breathe and heal, it will fester underneath or harden into a protective shell. By working through these exercises, we are beginning to heal that woundedness within you. Give yourself time to absorb these powerful steps of healing.

Now would be a good time to check in with your body. How are you feeling? Notice your breath—is it shallow or deep? Notice any tension that may exist. Breathe into those tight spaces seeking to release the tension. Offer a statement of gratitude for what you have been able to work through: your ability to look into yourself and your life gently, your ability to name those things that are no longer working for you, and your steps into releasing those things that are keeping you from the full, whole-hearted life you deserve.

Looking into the Light

So many beautiful elements exist within you. We don't want to overlook this. As my therapist said to me, "It is time to stop looking into the dark and look into the light." We are going to do a great deal of work claiming your future self, but for now, capture your thoughts on the light you see currently.

 Pause and complete Exercise 59.

What elements of strength do you see growing in you? Points of light?

_____

_____

_____

_____

_____

Where or when do you notice them?

_____

_____

_____

_____

_____

How do they tap into your best self?

_____

_____

_____

_____

_____

_____

> We all have been
> wounded to some
> degree. What we do
> with the woundedness
> defines us. If we learn
> and grow from it, it
> can be a catalyst.

> Mindfulness is
> critical because it
> helps you move at
> the healing pace
> that is right for you.

CHAPTER 12
Embracing Mindfulness

Mindfulness allows us to become aware of all those thoughts we carry, and we can choose to see them for what they are: our thoughts and not our essence.

You have done a great deal of work, and it is now time for a large breath. Earlier I asked you to check in with your breath and your body to see how you are doing. This is the beginning of mindfulness. "Mindfulness" is defined as "moment-by-moment awareness of thoughts, feelings, bodily sensations, and the surrounding environment" (Greater Good Science Center, n.d.). Mindfulness is paying attention to our thoughts and feelings and being curious about them and aware that they exist. How many times do we live in our heads without acknowledging the physical reactions we are having in our bodies or our feelings that stem from the situations around us? We have access to all this information, yet often we have been conditioned to stay in our well-worn patterns of thinking. With discipline and practice, our conscious minds can be taught the skill of effectively responding, as opposed to reacting.

As I share about mindfulness and encourage you to do it, I have to note that I am a work in progress. I created a life of being a "human doing" versus a "human being." If I wasn't striving in school or work, I was trying to do things to help others. Being still meant being idle, and that was a bad thing (my example of a limiting core belief). I couldn't even sit and watch TV without doing something at the same time (folding clothes, organizing something), or else I would consider myself "lazy." So you can imagine how the idea of "meditation" and being still for twenty . . . OK, even five minutes . . . would land on me. I also needed activity and to see immediate results with my workouts, so I would do aerobic classes and lift weights for maximum result. I resisted yoga and meditation for years. Who has the time, and how do you know if it is "working"?

I started taking a yoga class at the YMCA, and my yoga teacher wasn't just an instructor; he was a model for living. He explained how the pieces of yoga worked together and the connection of mind, body, and spirit. I had been working on all three separately and became fascinated with the idea of blending.

After years of denying my body, and my body periodically giving me a "wake-up" call like a panic attack, the idea of engaging it intentionally was intriguing. I learned that the focus starts with your breath and awareness of your body. I was aware of breathing techniques to calm down when you hyperventilate, but I didn't think of it as a way to engage in life. Yet breathing gets us "into" ourselves; it connects us intentionally. It is the start of mindfulness.

As I teach the course on leading retreats, one of the things I focus on in every class is to begin by "getting centered." We come into any room with a level of energy, and often it is frenetic. Whether it be the traffic on the way over, the action that wasn't completed before we left, or maybe even the conversation that didn't go as well as we would have liked, we all have things on our minds that may not serve us as we enter the next "space." Being able to slow down and regroup can help us engage in the way we want and be the people we want to be.

Getting centered begins with noticing your breath and, if it is rapid or shallow, seeking to breathe more deeply. It also means noticing any tension in your body so that you begin to release it. Often "breathing into" that part will help it relax. Many of us carry stress and tension in our shoulders and our foreheads. Just noticing that and bringing awareness will usually help you begin to release.

In the book, *The Untethered Soul: The Journey Beyond Yourself* (2007), Michael Singer says the best way to free yourself from the incessant chatter in your head is to step back and view it objectively. By just noticing it, you begin to realize that you are not the voice of the mind—you are just the one who hears it. Earlier, we checked in with your voice around some of the limiting beliefs that float around in your head. If you can see them for what they are, you can see when they are a waste of your time and energy.

In yoga, I heard a story of a man walking by a river with his young son. The son asked, "Father, is the river polluted?" The man answered, "No, the river is not polluted. The river is pure; it is just carrying pollution." That is how our minds are. Our minds are pure, but they can carry pollution at times. Mindfulness allows us to become aware of all those thoughts we carry, and we can choose to see them for what they are: our thoughts and not our essence. We can choose how much weight we give them and whether we will allow them space to travel with us. The voices inside our heads can get loud and active, which results in nervousness and negative energy. If you want to be free of these energies, you must allow them to pass through you instead of hiding them inside of you.

Embracing Mindfulness

Be still and simply watch for that part of you that feels a disturbance or tension. Notice if you can identify what is underneath. Could it be jealousy, an unmet need, or fear? As you notice this and perhaps understand what is leading to the feelings, do not go to judgement. Know that this is all part of our nature as human beings. As you pay attention, you can think about our earlier exercise and wonder: Where are you coming from? What are you trying to tell me? Are you speaking truth to me? As you detach from the feelings or body reactions, notice how this distance affects your experience. Maybe your breathing changes. Maybe you have less tension in your shoulders. Be curious and just notice.

The more you practice mindfulness and being able to rest in your body, the more you will be able to objectively see what is going on within and around you. You may even experience more peace and energy. You are releasing yourself to be more within your natural flow.

 Pause and complete Exercise 60.

Understanding mindfulness and how to begin developing that ability is an important step as we begin thinking about shifting out of the walls we have built around ourselves. We first have to notice them, notice what they feel like, notice the impact they are having, to make any kind of shift. Knowing this and doing this are two very different things. I have been trying to meditate in the morning for about ten years, and it can still be difficult to calm my mind. The achiever in me wants to master this practice and move on, but I have to remember the wisdom from another yoga instructor who says, "Years and inches." That is what it takes to move through your yoga "practice." You won't start out being able to stretch into some of the poses or hold other ones, but in time, you will. I believe this applies to all the life-shifting practices we are seeking to embrace.

The book *The Body Keeps the Score: Brain, Mind, and Body in the Healing of Trauma* talks about the fact that people who have experienced trauma can't get better unless they "know what they know and feel what they feel" (Van der Kolk, 2014). You can be fully in charge of your life only if you acknowledge the reality

Capture your thoughts or "voices."
What is swirling in your head at this moment?

Notice what is going on in your body and your breath.
Describe it and wonder to yourself, "What is that all about?"

What insight can you gain from this mindfulness exercise?

of your body. Mindfulness meditation and yoga are two ways to help us to notice our breath, which is one of the few body functions we can do both consciously and unconsciously. They help increase our ability to sense what is going on within and around us and to trust our inner knowing. As we pay attention to our bodies' sensations, we can recognize the ebb and flow of our emotions and increase our control over them.

Mindfulness is critical because it helps you move at the healing pace that is right for you. There may be times where you have to come to certain realizations before you are ready to move to the next step. Be patient and allow your inner self to emerge slowly.

I encourage you to practice mindfulness often. "Practice" is a good word to use because you have probably practiced other things in your life; maybe it was a particular sport or playing a musical instrument. With each of these things, it took time for it to feel natural and for you to feel "good at it."

 Pause and complete Exercise 61.

Practice Mindfulness

 Exercise 61

Find a quiet place where you will not be disturbed. Start by setting your phone timer for five minutes. Begin to breathe in slowly and deeply for a count of five. Feel the air expand your lungs and your stomach. Then release your breath slowly for a count of five. Do this three times. These are often called "cleansing breaths." Now, begin to notice where you feel tension. Can you release it? Notice the thoughts going through your head. Can you release them?

After your five minutes, capture what you noticed about this "practice."

_____

_____

_____

_____

_____

_____

_____

_____

_____

_____

_____

_____

_____

> **"**
> Getting centered
> begins with noticing
> your breath and, if it
> is rapid or shallow,
> seeking to breathe
> more deeply.
> **"**

> "It is now your turn
> to confidently
> walk through the
> door into your
> next chapter."

CHAPTER 13
Describing Your Desired Self

*It was powerful when my therapist said,
"Tambry, it is time to stop looking into the
dark and start looking into the light."*

Now we can move to the fun part: describing your desired self, writing your going-forward story, and capturing what you want for your main character. We have looked into the dark as we examined some limiting beliefs and sources of them; now it is time to look into the light!

I have shared that I spent years in therapy working through the layers of trauma and pain. To me, this important work—looking honestly at what has brought us to this place—is what brings us from victim to survivor. Like I mentioned around change management, it is important to understand your current state to be able to shift. Next you begin to envision the future you want to move toward. I began that move when my therapist said, "Tambry, it is time to stop looking into the dark and look into the light."

My next chapter included sharing more of myself with others. I found my voice and the courage to tell my story to those people close to me. Their validation of who I was and their affirmation of what I was seeking to do helped me move increasingly into my going-forward story. I could honestly claim that I was a "beloved child of God." These were not hollow words offered; they resonated within me. I began to confidently step through doors I had avoided in the past, claiming aspects of my whole self.

It is now your turn to confidently walk through the door into your next chapter. Review the notes that you have taken as you have worked through this book. Pull forward those things you want to claim for yourself.

Pause and complete Exercise 62.

We will explore your going-forward story in third-person singular point of view. Usually when we talk about ourselves, we speak in the first-person singular (I, me, my, mine, myself). In the third-person singular point of view, we speak of a separate person (she, her, hers, herself). The narrator describes the main character's thoughts and feelings about what is going on. I encourage you to write in third person because it helps you write more objectively as you describe what is happening to and within the main character (you).

As you move through the next exercise, continue to see yourself as the main character. For example, if you were reading the story of your life in a novel, what would the current chapter be called? What would this chapter be about? Try to capture a short summary of what is going on in this current chapter.

 Pause and complete Exercise 63.

What elements of strength do you see growing in you that you want to claim going forward?

_____

_____

_____

_____

How are you going to tap into your best self?

_____

_____

_____

What dreams and desires do you want to elaborate upon and bring forward?

_____

_____

_____

What reframed core beliefs do you want to make sure you pay attention to as you move into your new chapter? How can they be framed in a way to be life-giving?

_____

_____

_____

_____

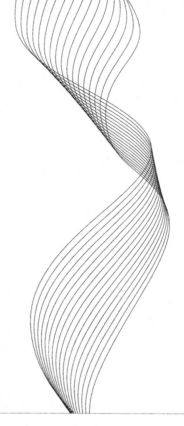

Have you gotten more accustomed to using all of yourself as you work through these sections? Are you **pausing** to see if your body or spirit wants you to add to what your mind had you write? Are you **breathing** as you reflect to check in on your inner knowing? Is your candle still lit?

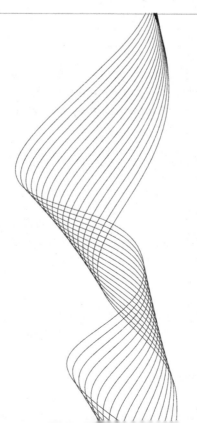

Capturing Your Story
Current chapter name:

Summary of chapter:

Now we will capture both the "outer" and "inner" story. For the outer story, briefly list the elements that comprise the character's current situation or objective circumstances, events, and facts. These are things that feel important to name and be aware of as you write your going-forward story. For me, the outer story was about a mom who wanted to claim her authentic life as she entered her third marriage. It was about her trying to be aware of mindsets that had previously gotten in her way and making decisions about the work that she did, the activities she engaged in, and the supportive friends with whom she surrounded herself. She found herself entering the second half of her life and wanting to claim a new trajectory and bravely find her voice around her story to help others.

 Pause and complete Exercise 64.

List the elements of your outer story. Exercise 64

Let's move to your inner story. This includes listing all the elements you want to capture about what is going on inside you. Also, try to capture the emotional experience and interpretation of your outer story (thoughts and feelings you have about what is going on around you). This would be a good time to check in with your body and what it is telling you to focus on. For me, the inner story was about a woman who had a story to tell but was concerned about how to share it with the important people around her. It was also about the fear of people looking at her differently as she shared the whole of her life and her experience. These feelings were countered with the feeling of certainty and the conviction of what she knew she needed to do.

Pause and complete Exercise 65.

List the elements of your inner story.   Exercise 65

As you look at the two descriptions (the elements of the outer and inner stories), notice which one you assigned more importance. What can be added to better balance the two? What more can you capture or say?

To catch the mood and tone of your story so far, circle all the words and phrases connected to your outer and inner story that suggest a negative mood or tone. What do you notice?

Pause and complete Exercise 66.

Describe the prevailing mood and tone of your story.　**Exercise 66**

Consider what different word choices might improve mood. For your outer story, consider which details you might emphasize more or de-emphasize to change the mood and tone.

Pause and complete Exercise 67.

What word choices would improve the mood? What details do you want to emphasize more or de-emphasize to change the mood?

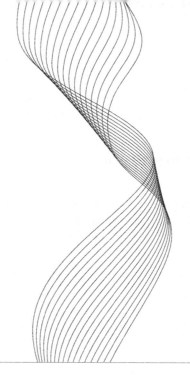

Are you continuing to tap into the whole of you as you are processing? I have been asking you to do a great deal of thinking and analyzing. To get you ready for our next step, take an intentional moment to **get quiet and into your body.** If you would like, this would be a good time to do one of your meditation practices where you get in touch with your body and spirit.

In the stillness, what are you sensing about your story? What do you know you want to capture? What is essential for you to claim in your going-forward story?

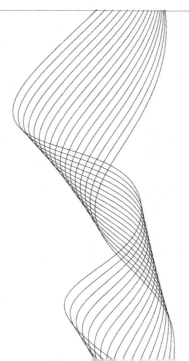

Are you ready to rewrite your story and capture your current chapter from a different angle? What is the essence you want to capture for your going-forward chapter name?

 Pause and complete Exercise 68.

Going-forward chapter name: Exercise 68

_____

_____

_____

(Tip: This title doesn't have to be succinct. You could simply list all the words you want to describe it.)

Now rewrite your chapter synopsis or summary. **Describe this chapter with an ending that leaves you inspired.** As you write, make sure to capture both your inner and outer stories. Again, use your journal to give you space beyond what is provided in this book.

 Pause and complete Exercise 69.

Summary of chapter:

As you think about fleshing out your chapter and story, do you need to learn or understand anything about the situation? Maybe you are curious about some things regarding other people in the story or even within yourself? In the absence of data or information, we will always make up stories. It's how we are wired and goes back to our most primitive survival. Many times, when we actually check into "facts" a little more, we can be pleasantly surprised that we misjudged people or situations.

 Pause and complete Exercise 70.

Let's go back to change management theory. Once we have envisioned and moved toward our desired future state, it is important to put things into place to help us stay there. I previously mentioned the "unfreeze – change – refreeze" framework. Let's take some time to think about what might increase the likelihood that you maintain this envisioned state and continue in this thriving place. I am sure you know that these kinds of changes are not quick or easy, and they require a great deal of support.

To tap back into my change journey, my body, mind, and spirit all told me that I was ready to shed the old limiting beliefs and story. I had gone through the "unfreezing" and was ready to let go of my old state. I had done the work to grow a clear image of the identity I wanted to claim (created a line of sight and moved toward the desired state). Finally, I had a core group of friends who listened, helped me process, and cheered me on as I made the move. I now have an unconditionally loving partner who undergirds my every step and helps me speak to the unhealthy messages or fears that come up to impede me. My support system allows me to be vulnerable, grow my confidence, stretch myself, and be excited at the new freedom I am experiencing. They stood witness to my growth into my reclaimed self, one who lives authentically, feels worthy, and stands tall without fear to encourage others to claim their light and their stories (my new "refrozen" state).

As you think about the changes in your life that you want to embrace, it is critical to think through those elements of support for you. The first things to identify are your supporting characters and resources. Who are those people in your life who will be champions for you as you seek to grow in this new space? Who can you go to when the limiting beliefs crop up to help you see them for what they are? Think about what each person can do to support you and what

What do you need to learn and understand more about your situation?

_____

_____

_____

_____

_____

What do you need to learn and understand more about other people in the story?

_____

_____

_____

_____

_____

What do you need to learn and understand more about yourself?

_____

_____

_____

_____

_____

specific steps you, the main character, will take to get this support from your supporting characters.

 Pause and complete Exercise 71.

We have also talked about the importance of nurturing your whole self: mind, body, and spirit. Think about how you defined each of these earlier. What can you do in each area to help ensure you stay the course as you claim your going-forward story? Remember that you are worth it!

Name three people, resources, or "supporting characters" for you and what you need from them: **Exercise 71**

1) _____

2) _____

3) _____

What immediate steps will you take to garner support?

1) _____

2) _____

3) _____

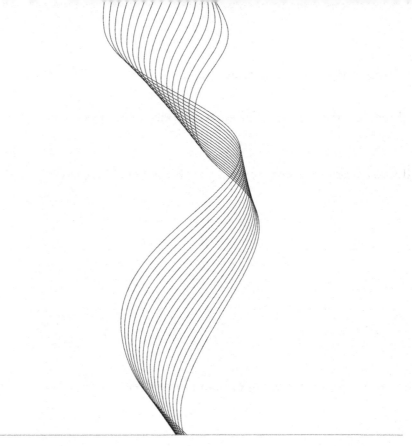

This is a good time once more to **pause** and consider the whole of you and make sure your body and spirit are being heard for this next exercise.

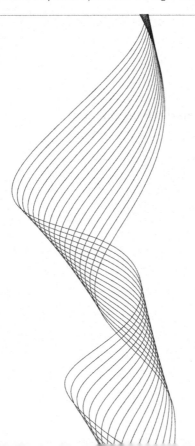

Pause and complete Exercise 72.

Name three specific practices for each category to help you stay the course.

Exercise 72

Mind (for example, readings, reminders, affirmations, journal)

_____

_____

_____

_____

_____

_____

Body (for example, exercise, yoga, being in nature)

_____

_____

_____

_____

_____

_____

Spirit (for example, prayers, meditation, stillness)

_____

_____

_____

_____

_____

_____

> In the absence of data
> or information, we
> will always make up
> stories. It's how we
> are wired and goes
> back to our most
> primitive survival.

"

Many broken
people are in this
world, and not
everyone in your life
will be ready and/or
willing to embrace
and support your
authentic self.
That is OK.

"

CHAPTER 14
Claiming Your Going-Forward Story

*As I began to claim my going-forward story,
it was important to keep practicing mindfulness
to see both what doors were being opened and
when limiting beliefs jumped in to sabotage.*

My last step to move from survivor to thriver was to unearth what was holding me back from completely being seen and feeling strength in my story. This was the new identity I wanted to claim. My reimagined self was one who was open to see her worthiness, willing to be seen by others and to connect on a heart level with those around her.

After going through the process of reflecting on myself, raising awareness at every level about my limiting beliefs and my old story, I really thought that I was done. I was ready to help others using all my skills and self-knowledge. I was ready to lead retreats and do individual coaching. I reached out to many supporters, communicated the availability of these resources widely, and yet had very minimal response. What I did have were requests for me to come speak. My limiting belief said, "I'm a facilitator, not the main show. I help others grow by leading them through the process, not by exposing myself." Putting myself and my story out there on stage, literally, would be another trajectory-setting decision.

With discernment and intentional steps, I did it. As I shared my story, my eyes connected with others in the audience who were engaged in my words. After my talk, many came up to me. One woman said, "Your story is my story. You were made to do this work of encouraging healing." Another woman came up to me beside herself with excitement. She told me that she had been feeling nudges to take a step forward out of just surviving, and hearing my story gave her the confidence to do that. I am grateful I chose to allow my voice to be heard.

A reality that survivors must recognize even when they are moving into thriving is that not everyone will be supportive. If someone has not done their healing work, they may not be ready to support you. They may be threatened by this stronger version of you, and that is their work to do. You do not need to allow their limitations to put boundaries around you. I mentioned earlier how often people will want to protect the perpetrator because of that person's position in the family or community. That is alright. That may be part of your outer story, but you can choose how much emphasis it receives. You can also manage your inner story around it. You can set healthy boundaries so that the foundation you have established does not get eroded away.

 Pause and complete Exercise 73.

Building on the wound metaphor, we can explore this healing and claiming process a little more. We have to recognize that it takes time. You may find times when it seems better or at least easier to cover over some of the wounds. My experience is that under that cover, they will often fester. If you look up the definition of "fester," you will see words like rot, poison, irritation, bitterness, inflammation, and corrupt. Who wants any of that going on within their bodies and souls? We may think we are being strong by sealing our wounds away, but it takes light and air to allow them to truly heal.

I recently had skin surgery on my shin. The surgeon told me this was a tricky place to heal given the reduced blood flow. It ended up also being a big issue because the skin over the shin is such a tight area, and I have a condition that impacts the skin's healing. I had been through several of these surgeries earlier in the year, and I was tired of the recovery period that kept me from exercising. I thought I had given enough time to let the wound heal and ended up tearing my stitches from too much activity. This led to a very lengthy healing process. I learned more about my body through this experience, which reinforced that I must not push myself too far. Patience is required in the healing.

The scar will always be visible, and that is OK. It represents part of what I have been through and part of what I have learned. It is an outward sign of what I wish to be, a wounded healer whose life experiences can be a light and a reminder that we are always in the process of learning and healing. As we look at our scars, they remind us of the journeys we have been on and what lies before us.

What might get in the way of you living into your going-forward story (people, circumstances, even unaddressed limiting beliefs)?

_____

_____

_____

_____

_____

_____

_____

What can you do to address these things?

_____

_____

_____

_____

_____

_____

How might you be prepared if/when they come up?

_____

_____

_____

_____

_____

_____

Pause and complete Exercise 74.

Reflect on the wound and scar metaphor. What does it bring up for you?

Exercise 74

What have your learned from the past healing of physical wounds?

What insights do you need to keep in mind as you seek to heal your internal wounds?

Remember the "chipping away a sculpture" analogy I shared earlier? We are each a piece of stone or clay, and we are also the sculptor taking away pieces that are not part of who we are meant to be. Much of the transformation may have occurred already, but opportunities are always available to grow a little more and chip away that which is not meant to be. Our journeys continue as we evolve how we think and act and claim that which is truly aligned with our essences. That may mean refining who we are, what we believe, what we want for our lives, and whom we choose to walk the path with us. It means consciously deciding to live our lives in health and harmony, seeking the highest good in ourselves and others.

You will see yourself changing and patterns beginning to shift. Capture these shifts as they happen. This will serve as encouragement to you when you run into people or situations that seem to thwart your thriving spirit.

Pause and complete Exercise 75.

Capture the changing patterns you are noticing. **Exercise 75**

All stories include antagonists, the people, things, or situations that seem to work against the main character. I have said how important it is to anticipate barriers and have a plan to address what may eat away at your established base. But what if that antagonist is you? Those limiting beliefs will creep back in when you are not looking. Let me share how this happened to me.

My current husband and I had been dating about six months (the second time, after our twenty-one-year "break") and were at a very romantic restaurant when my limiting belief was triggered. I had shared something that made me feel vulnerable, and his response hooked into my feelings of unworthiness and mandatory self-sufficiency. I threw up my walls and had a huge internal dialogue going on in my head: "Fine, I don't need you. I can do this by myself. I shouldn't have trusted you anyway. You are now officially cut off from my emotions and my heart." What this looked like on the outside was stone silence. You have probably heard of fight or flight reactions. In this situation, I didn't attack him in fight mode or storm out in flight mode. I sat in "freeze" mode and stuffed my feelings down like I had so expertly learned to do. Interestingly, we had a similar conversation over the phone twenty-one years ago about our status as a couple. My stone silence then and later hanging up with no resolution or discussion resulted in our break up back then.

Thankfully, this time I recognized what was going on and made a different choice to take a different action. I looked at him and said, "The wall just went up, and I can tell I am closing you off." This was a bridge that allowed us to talk through what might have broken us up. I allowed myself to be vulnerable and honest about what was going on within me. My mindfulness work showed me that I was walling myself off, and I knew I did not like that feeling. My breathing work gave me space to be able to choose how I responded and to move into the person I wanted to be—open and authentic. His positive response to this reinforced what it can look like when you trust and allow your true self to be seen. We were married a year and a half later.

One word of wisdom that Brené Brown shares is that you need to be discerning with whom you allow to witness your vulnerability. Many broken people are in this world, and not everyone in your life will be ready and/or willing to embrace and support your authentic self. That is OK. You have identified your supporting characters and your resources. These are the people who will be the fertile ground from which you can grow and blossom.

> "My breathing work gave me space to be able to choose how I responded and to move into the person I wanted to be—open and authentic."

"
As you become a
stronger version of
yourself, you can
be an inspiration to
others. You, too, can
be a lightkeeper.
"

CHAPTER 15
Growing

We are never done with our growth, and that is actually good. We can always write more chapters. God continues to surprise me with what my story is becoming; it is much bigger than I ever thought it could be.

Now I turn back to my story to share my growth and gratitude with the hope it will encourage you. I believe sharing is the doorway through which we discover and impart our special gifts and abilities. In return, we gain self-worth and feel affirmed for who we truly are. As I have shared these parts of me, things unique to me and my story, I have gained an understanding of the breadth and depth of what God intended for me. This feels so much better than trying to prove myself in a calculated way given the world's values, which can be skewed. Wouldn't it be incredible if we all could live out of our authenticity, draw upon the best of ourselves, and feel appreciated for just that very thing? As we seek to do this, we see ourselves continue to unfold, discovering new gifts and abilities we didn't know were there.

Growth

As we pursue our visions of what will lead us toward wholeness, fulfillment, and a sense of rightness in life, we will receive two gifts: self-insight and the process of getting there. In my process of "getting there," I heard a song called "Broken Vessels (Amazing Grace)" (Houston & Myrin, 2014). This song was helpful to me as it described us all—people who have been broken and scattered at some point in our lives. But then we are mended, and in our new forms, we can see more clearly the lives we are meant to live. With the brokenness, light comes through the cracks of our vessels for all to see the beauty within.

I am a vessel nearly mended. I would not have the depth of understanding to offer if I had not been through the breaking and the healing. I think about some of those items in our houses that may be in perfect condition, and we are afraid to use them or even touch them. These things are so precious, we don't want to do anything that would take away the sheen of perfection. Yet what good are they if not used? I love the phrase "our mess is our message." Another way I have heard it said: focus on what you yearn for and let that be your purpose and meaning.

Early in this book, I shared that my young heart always cheered for the underdog and the marginalized. At that time in my life, I didn't see that it was the hurt part of me wanting to reach the hurt part in others. My growth has allowed me to find a way to stand up for justice, speak out, and in my own way begin to stop the silence and secrecy around sexual abuse.

I was recently asked to speak at a fundraiser for a child abuse resource center. The invitation came the way many doors have opened for me: I met someone in an unlikely setting who connected me to a need and opportunity. I always try to be open to those nudges to step out and expand myself and my message. As I left this talk to 500 loving souls who sought to support the marginalized children in their community, my heart was light, and tears welled in my eyes. The song "Happy" by Pharrell Williams came on the radio, and I could feel the little girl inside me dancing. She was grateful that she could make a difference, be seen, be heard, and be appreciated. For her to be part of this movement of hope—to give a voice to the children who may not be able to articulate what is happening to them—was huge! She could see how we were making a difference and hopefully saving some children from pain and hurt. If nothing else, we were helping in the healing.

So have I achieved self-actualization? I see moments of it, and other times I find myself back in the self-doubting place. The nice thing is that I am able to navigate those times much more effectively and quickly.

As I was in the finishing stages of writing this book, I found myself being pressed to quantify and state the timing of when results would be seen from my efforts. This triggered me for a couple of reasons. First, much of what I was doing was God-led, and in that realm, you never know the timing or even the results. You trust that your efforts will have impact. The second piece tapped into my "achiever" who had not felt as successful as she wanted. The retreats did not take off like I had hoped. My outreach to speak at universities had not been fruitful. What if my efforts around this book fail? I believe there is a need, and I want to help people, but what if my efforts and my writing are not enough? Am I worthy of such an effort? Should I stay small and not share my voice? I am usually positive and light, but that night was very dark for me. As I journaled into the late hours, I worked through these feelings. I ended by writing, "I believe I am supposed to do this, and I know the rewards and outgrowth may take time." I then wrote, "God, what do you want me to know?" My Companions group had been talking about the importance of getting quiet and listening to God. As I sat, using my mindfulness practice, I heard, "Stay the course." That was enough to give me peace and to go to sleep.

The next morning, I was reading my devotional, which talked about how growth comes with a roller coaster of emotions and how none of them are wrong, just part of the journey. We need to embrace them and see what they have to teach us. We must trust that defeating feelings will pass and joy will return. Then, in large bold words it said, "Stay the Course." I felt like God was putting an exclamation point on what I heard the night before. I also began to realize that those things I listed as "failures" were not. Lives were touched with every outreach I made. My confidence was built with each speaking engagement and retreat I led, and my story became clearer and fed the content of this book. I am once again reminded that personal growth is a journey and not a destination.

Pause and complete Exercise 76.

How do you see your growth continuing?   Exercise 76

Growing in Gratitude

Experts say that gratitude is key to a happy life. As I wrote this book, overwhelming feelings of gratitude blended with a sense of joy and peace. I reflected on the people around me who each played a unique supporting role. It has been a painful journey—mentally, emotionally, and physically—but the persons of light who surrounded me gave me hope and encouragement. Healing takes time and patience, which has always been difficult for me, so that is all the more reason to surround myself with the compassion, love, and support of others.

I want you also to have a support system like this: people who can know, love, and support your whole self. As we open ourselves up to others, we have to accept that we don't have to have it all together and probably never will. At the same time, we don't have to be alone in our imperfection. I hope you can join me in realizing we don't have to hold it all together for others. We just need to be our authentic selves.

 Pause and complete Exercise 77.

As I worked on finishing this book, the sadness of loss and death was all around me. I opened my story by describing one death after the other. Now, within a month, I experienced the loss of one of my dear Companions as well as my sweet furry companion of more than twelve years. Both precious souls loved me in their own ways through very difficult chapters of my life. The gratitude I can express is that, through my journey, I have become more equipped to move through this period of sadness and loss. When my friend died, I invited the Companions over to my home to share our sadness together. I didn't feel that there was anything to do per se; I just wanted to create a space for us to be in the moment together, to share our love for one another and for our beloved friend. We used our time to plan a celebration of life to meet our needs for saying goodbye. To honor the multifaceted nature of our group and our friend, we all wore "bling" that we knew would make her smile, we brought pictures of our times together, we shared songs and writings that spoke of our feelings for her, we laughed, and we cried. As much as I miss her, this heart-felt tribute brought me peace and closure. We continue to honor her by talking about her in our weekly meeting. We reflect on how she touches our lives and hearts daily as we think of things she would have said, done, or shared with us. She continues to make the chapters of our lives richer.

To whom are you grateful?

_____

_____

_____

_____

_____

What would you specifically want them to know?

_____

_____

_____

_____

_____

What do you intentionally want to do to be vulnerable around these people and let them love you?

_____

_____

_____

_____

_____

_____

_____

For you pet owners, you know that the loss of an animal is like losing a family member. My sweet dog was such a part of everything I did. I was mindful of meeting my needs and the needs of my family as we said goodbye to her. I have taken mindful actions that helped me feel the loss but also heal. I have needed to change up my routines because she was such a part of them. I have found a way to create a remembrance spot for her on my counter, so my heart can be touched by the sweet cards I have received from friends sending me encouragement. I am claiming what I need.

For me, healing means taking all the goodness, love, and light I received from these two precious souls and holding them in my heart and channeling them in my life. It means being vulnerable in claiming what I need at this time and trusting that loved ones around me will understand and support me. I am building on my continued growth and learning to receive.

I hope that you too will sense hope, joy, and peace as you claim your growth and healing, as you claim your going-forward story. Capture those times when you feel abundance. That memory will help carry you on days that are not as bright or easy.

Lightkeepers

My dream and desire are to be present for those who are hurting and give them a safe place to share their stories, explore their feelings, and feel close to God. I want to break the cycle of abuse and evil by providing each individual a place to explore healing and not harbor the pain and resentment that can come out in destructive ways. I want to create a genuine community with the characteristics of trust, vulnerability, authenticity, support, and unconditional love. An image came to me of creating a safe nest for delicate birds that helps them awaken to the light within them. I envision tenderly holding and encouraging the bird, not trying to help it fly high; when it is ready to fly, it will do so. I just need to stand in the gap of healing and growth, to create a container and a nest for those who need it.

When I founded Going Forward: Survivors to Thrivers, I wanted to have a website to give encouragement and resources to others. This would serve somewhat as a "nest" where people could land and find the comfort they needed. When building a website, the first thing you do is determine a domain name to purchase. As I reflected on my desire to start a movement and build a community, focusing on the plural of who we are made sense. We are survivorstothrivers.com, a group who wants to encourage and empower other survivors of sexual abuse to move into thriving.

In this book, I walked you through exercises to help you "refreeze" into your new desired state. I want you to be able to live into your going-forward story, but I know that limiting beliefs can be tricky. Outside forces can work their way in, and unfortunate experiences will happen. That is why our website will be very valuable to you. As you think about continuing your growth into thriving, I encourage you to visit our semimonthly blog. On the first of each month, we offer encouragement on your journey. On the fifteenth of each month, we provide exercises to grow your whole self—mind, body, and spirit. We also invite you to comment and share with other survivors who are seeking support.

My next statement will date this book forever. The world has just begun to deal with the effects of the novel coronavirus COVID-19. We are all trying to figure out what isolating ourselves—to be part of the solution and not part of the problem—looks like. Yet in this isolation, we seek ways not to be isolated. There are so many ways to connect and support one another virtually. This week, every one of my meetings moved to virtual space, either through FaceTime, Skype, or Zoom. Friends, family, and neighbors shared how they were doing and asking what they could do to help one another. As hard as all of this is, it is showing us the power of a virtual community.

We invite you to be a part of our virtual community at survivorstothrivers. com that seeks to bring light into the darkness that surrounds sexual abuse. We are all in different places of the continuum as we move from survivor to thriver, but each voice and each journey is valuable. We want to hear your thoughts and your inspirational stories. We want to hear about your light. **As you become a stronger version of yourself, you can be an inspiration to others. You, too, can be a lightkeeper.**

As I have worked with other survivors, the thing that most impresses me is the willingness to be there for one another. There is something special about people who self-select into a group seeking spiritual depth, closeness, camaraderie, vulnerability, and a willingness to learn and support one another in this growth. **Let's all shine on and move from surviving to thriving together!**

What's Next?

I hope that this book has been meaningful to you. As I wrote it, I thought about the women out there who needed to hear encouragement and have a loving guide to move into a whole-hearted, thriving life. When reviewers would tell me of the tears shed, the openings found, the parallels experienced, and the tools they would utilize, my heart soared. That was why I wrote the book!

So what's next? I would welcome you to:

- **Contact me.** I would love to hear how this book has touched your heart, your life, your story. As you share these things, you give me encouragement to keep my outreach going, and I believe it will help you feel the freedom of using your voice to speak your truth. You can contact me at tambry@survivorstothrivers.com.

- **Review the book.** To help others know of this resource, please leave reviews on Goodreads and Amazon. My hope is that the book can be a catalyst to an awakening the light movement where we shine light into the darkness that surrounds sexual abuse all over this world.

- **Join our community of thrivers.** Visit our website and follow our social media channels. (We also want you to "like" us!) These channels were established to provide support, offer encouragement, and foster a loving community that understands. We are available to you as you work through this book and even on the other side of this healing step if you find challenges from limiting beliefs or other antagonists as you seek to thrive. We hope you will reach out to us, so we can help empower you on this journey.

Much love,
Tambry

- 🌐 survivorstothrivers.com
- ✉ tambry@survivorstothrivers.com
- f survivorstothriversofficial
- 🅞 survivorstothrivers
- 🐦 GFS2T

Going Forward
Survivors to Thrivers

References

Allender, D. B. (2016). *Healing the Wounded Heart: The Heartache of Sexual Abuse and the Hope of Transformation*. Grand Rapids, MI: Baker Books.

Brown, B. (2012). *Daring Greatly: How the Courage to Be Vulnerable Transforms the Way We Live, Love, Parent, and Lead.* New York, NY: Gotham Books.

Centers for Disease Control and Prevention. (2020, April 13). *About the CDC-Kaiser Ace Study*. From Centers for Disease Control and Prevention: https://www.cdc.gov/violenceprevention/childabuseandneglect/acestudy/about.html

Felitti, V. J., et al. (1998). Relationship of Childhood Abuse and Household Dysfunction to Many of the Leading Causes of Death in Adults: The Adverse Childhood Experiences (ACE) Study. *American Journal of Preventative Medicine,* 14(4), 245-258.

Greater Good Science Center. (n.d.). What Is Mindfulness? Retrieved May, 2020 from Greater Good Magazine: https://greatergood.berkeley.edu/topic/mindfulness/definition

Houston, J., & Myrin, J. (2014). Broken Vessels (Amazing Grace) [Recorded by Hillsong Worship].

Maslow, A. (1943). A Theory of Human Motivation. *Psychological Review*, 50(3), 370-396.

Nouwen, H. J. M. (1972). *The Wounded Healer: Ministry in Contemporary Society.* New York, NY: Knopf Doubleday Publishing Group.

Riley, B. E. (1999). *Building Community, Relationships, Competency: Learning through Peer Feedback*. Elsie Y. Cross Associates Inc.

Rupp, J. (2008). *Open the Door: A Journey to the True Self*. Notre Dame, IN: Sorin Books.

Singer, M. A. (2007). *The Untethered Soul: The Journey Beyond Yourself.* Oakland, CA: New Harbinger Publications, Inc.

The Chopra Center (2013). Getting Unstuck: Creating a Limitless Life [Streaming video] [Recorded by D. Chopra, & O. Winfrey]. Carlsbad, CA.

Van der Kolk, B. A. (2014). *The Body Keeps the Score: Brain, Mind, and Body in the Healing of Trauma*. New York, NY: Penguin Books.

About the Author

Tambry Harris is a leadership and life coach, survivor of childhood sexual abuse, and founder of **Going Forward: Survivors to Thrivers**, an organization that provides individual guidance, retreats, and speaking engagements to bring awareness and light into the shame, silence, and darkness that surrounds sexual abuse. Tambry has a master's degree in applied psychology and certifications in leadership coaching, spiritual direction, diversity, and change management.

After spending sixteen years in corporate America, Tambry created her own coaching practice to help individuals enhance their effectiveness and claim lives of significance. She found her voice, named her truth, and created a vision around how she could help others who have experienced the pain and shame of sexual abuse to find healing, strength, and freedom. Through her book, *Awakening the Light*, she shares her inspiring journey of moving from survivor to thriver and creating the Going Forward movement. Her dream is that survivors of sexual abuse will no longer be trapped by fear and limitations from their old stories and can claim whole-hearted, life-giving, going-forward stories.

She married the love of her life, Randy, in 2017 and has a daughter from a previous marriage and two stepsons.

Fun Fast Facts
- **Favorite vacation:** anywhere in the mountains or by the coast
- **Hometown:** the Queen City (Charlotte, North Carolina)
- **Favorite exercise:** cardio dance, yoga, and long hikes to beautiful waterfalls
- **Dream home:** on the water facing west for sunsets
- **Favorite 1980s band:** Journey

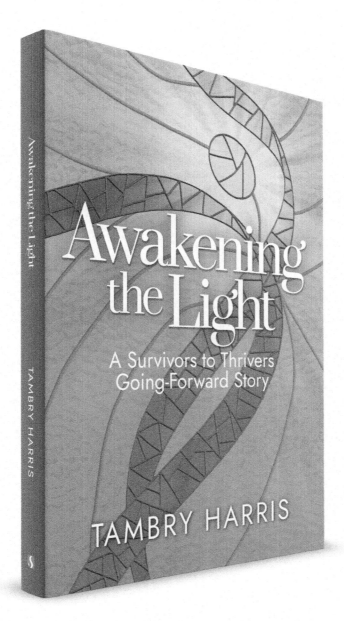

🌐 survivorstothrivers.com

✉ tambry@survivorstothrivers.com

f survivorstothriversofficial

📷 survivorstothrivers

🐦 GFS2T

 Going Forward
Survivors to Thrivers

Made in the USA
Columbia, SC
05 October 2020